I0618043

Shut Up and Listen: Me vs. Me

Confessions of a Bipolar Rock and Roller

Rob McCuen

Edited and Designed by Paul J. Hoffman

PathBinder
Publishing LLC
COLUMBUS, INDIANA

Copyright © 2023 by Rob McCuen

Cover image: Rudy and Peter Skitterians from Pixabay
Back cover image: Michael Dober

All rights reserved. This book or any portion thereof may not be reproduced or used in any manner whatsoever without the express written permission of the publisher except for the use of brief quotations in a book review or scholarly journal.

First Printing: 2020

ISBN 978-1-955088-65-7

PathBinder Publishing LLC
P.O. Box 2611
Columbus, IN 47202

Contents

Foreword I

When I first met Rob McCuen, he was beating the skins for an awesome power pop band called Red Ball Jets at Zak's on the east side of Milwaukee in the early 1980s. The brash drummer, along with his bandmates, were part of the city's burgeoning new wave/punk/power pop music scene. I was infected by the band's hard-driving power pop sounds, and had intended on seeing Red Ball Jets again.

Unfortunately, that didn't happen, although I still have my cherished Red Ball Jets "Rockin'" EP. I followed several other area bands throughout the '80s, but never ended up at another gig in with Rob McCuen was playing.

Flash forward nearly three decades. I'd moved to Indiana, gotten married for the second time, had a mess of kids, was almost 25 years into what turned into a 34-year journalism career, and joined Facebook (it was better back then). Through this social medium, I reconnected with all sort of people from various parts of my past lives, including Rob McCuen. Most of Rob's efforts during that time were spent as a rogue musician, keeping the beat and/or signing for acts such as RPMs, Plasticland, Liquid Pink, Dog-Style Dandies, The Carolinas, White-Hot Tizzies, Love Bully, and Rob McCuen and the Ruins. He's now played on 23 records, gigged in 29 states and 14 countries and earned a reputation as one of the Milwaukee music scene's more controversial members.

Rob and I chatted about music and a shared interest in car racing. He had written a lot about short-track racing, and as a sports writer in Indiana, I'd covered the same. We decided to meet up again on one of my trips back to Milwaukee, where he planned to play an open jam at Caroline's Jazz Club over Christmas. When my wife, brother, sister-in-law and I got there, the door was locked. Apparently, they didn't do the open jams over Christmas. Oh, well. When Rob showed up, we drove to Bay View, had a couple of beers and shot the bull at some place on KK.

Ten years after those beers, he asked me if I'd edit a book he was writing — a bunch of stories about his life, as well as some of his lyrics. Why not? I got out of the journalism thing in September 2019, set my sights on finishing my third book, and was open to taking on editing and writing jobs.

So, I did my best to fix Rob's punctuation and spelling, although some words are spelled incorrectly on purpose; it's a street thing, I'm told. Other than that, what you're reading is what Rob sent me. It's what he wanted to tell the world. So, if you have issues with any of it, take it up with him.

What lies herein isn't pretty. It's a raw, unflinching, unadulterated, undeterred, examination of the life of a fighter — someone who not only has fought the manic ups and paralyzing downs of bipolar I disorder, but also someone who has fought his own raging anger, uncontrolled desires, and a fear of showing any fear. He's also fought those who are closest to him and love him the most, and he has also fought himself.

Me vs. Me. Rob vs. Rob. Mano a mano. Which Rob will win in the end? That's a question that only Rob McCuen can ultimately answer.

He asks you to Shut Up and Listen to what he has to say.

Hopefully, you'll get something out of the ride you're about to undertake. As you read this book, feel free to take mental health breaks, a nice walk, put on some rain forest tunes and imagine yourself floating peacefully on a light, fluffy cloud in an azure sky, the sun's warmth gently caressing you. You're gonna need it.

Paul J. Hoffman
March 2020

Foreword II

When I first moved to Milwaukee, as a writer and photographer, I had a photo series going where I asked people to "model food." Later this became known as "Vogueing," but this was back in the late '80s, and Madonna had not yet coined the term.

I'd gone with my friends to the local grocery store on Milwaukee's East Side to take pictures posing with broccoli, yogurt and cans of Vienna sausages. There was a guy noticing us from a distance who obviously was saying "WTH" to himself. So, I approached him, grabbed something out of the frozen foods bin, and said, "You want in? I'm taking pictures of people posing with food," and thrust a box of Birdseye frozen peas into his hands. To my surprise, he complied, albeit with a eye-roll-punctuated, what-IS-going-on-here look on his face.

A couple of days later, after I'd processed the film and looked over some proofs, my roommate saw the frozen peas pic and commented, "Oh, that guy? He's an asshole." I asked her how she knew him, what was his name, etc. "Rob McCuen. He's in a bunch of bands, like Liquid Pink."

It turned out that Liquid Pink was the kind of band I was looking for, and that McCuen played drums in a variety of the kinds of bands I'd always loved: power pop, garage, psychedelic, theatrical glam — and that the kinds of people who played these mostly underground genres tended to be charismatic, center-of-attention seeking, type-A characters. In other words — depending on your perspective — assholes.

By that definition, I'm pretty much an asshole myself, so it was no wonder that Rob and I crossed paths many times in the following years, becoming acquaintances as I wrote about and shot local underground bands (and for a while there, fronted one of my own), and eventually evolved into a friendship that has miraculously survived our mutual egos and stubbornness.

And part of that was due to my fandom of his work: not only as drummer for some of my favorite Milwaukee bands (the aforementioned garage pop of Liquid Pink and the psychedelic blast of Plasticland), but as drummer and often frontman of his own acts: Love Bully, a snappy muscle of a cock-rock band; The White Hot Tizzies, full of Midwestern melodic punk; and just Rob McCuen and the Ruins. All three bands featured his hooky songwriting, constantly torn up and put back together as he went through personnel and theme changes with his bands with song titles like "Life Imitates Art," "Brains in a Jar," and his paean to one of his favorite sportsmen, "I'm AJ Foyt," which lands more like a projection of himself into an open wheel car rather than simple tribute.

What I did not understand until the more recent years of our friendship was that Rob suffered (and continues to suffer) from bipolar disorder, a condition I was not at all familiar with until recently. I just chalked up what I now know as his manic or depressive phases as just him being an asshole.

About a dozen years back, I went to a White Hot Tizzies gig in a small club and was one of very few people there. I wasn't aware that his beloved mother was not doing well, and in retrospect, that he was likely having a manic episode that was crashing into depression. He chose to take it out on his audience, lobbing insults at the handful of people nursing their watered-down drinks, translating what is normally a cocksure stage presence worthy of David Lee Roth into his contempt for the whole situation. It wasn't pretty, and when I reviewed the show in my blog I said so, literally and publicly lecturing him for six long paragraphs.

"He's not going to take this well," a mutual friend advised me, and I knew it. I was anticipating the eventual backlash. I was ready for him to go for my jugular in fury — as a fellow Saggitarian, I knew how precisely a wounded archer could still shoot and was bracing for the verbal hit. Instead, he did not. With clarity, he admitted I was right in my review, stepped back, gathered his thoughts and moved on, friendship intact. Rob McCuen has a lot of balls (sometimes too much), but in cases like this, it takes a lot of those balls to admit a mistake, or worse, defeat.

This wasn't the only time he's pissed me — and others who care about him — off. But, we put up with it because we know he has that capacity to re-evaluate, and re-work himself as well as his songs, his stories, his art to incorporate his lessons learned, and when his stubbornness gives way to growth, it's a glorious thing. It's why I've trusted him with teaching my son the basics of rock and roll drumming. It's why I still answer the phone when he calls, hours after he's insulted me in spinning denial of a manic episode. It's why I'm even writing this foreword for this collection of stories from across his life and passions.

I've seen these stories in various forms, and each time they got polished a little more with the experiences he's gone through. I'm not convinced some of these aren't embellished, but Rob's not a journalist, he's a storyteller concerned with setting a scene, and then taking the reader along with it on a tour of music, sports, or just growing up in the Iowa cornfields, from the perspective of an underground denizen.

You, the reader, will just have to accept that your tour guide — as erudite and knowledgeable as he is — is bipolar. So, sometimes he'll go off topic. Sometimes he'll outright piss you off. But this is a tour of the Midwest off the beaten path, and your tour guide has been to hell (and heaven) and back and lived to tell the tale. Let him tell it.

Veronica Rusnak
March 2020

Preface

AND THE WEAPONS WERE WORDS

Wanna piss me off? Call me a poet. Fuck poets. Kerouac was a poet and look what happened to him. "On the Road," my ass. When he wasn't out chasing his warped beat-dreams, the fucking bum was living in his mother's basement. So, I know what I'm up against, and I have no illusions. As human beings, poets are by and large a bunch of self-absorbed (well, there's one thing we have in common), drunkie/junkie assholes, whining about their muses and romanticizing their lowly lots in life.

I don't wanna hear it, not that I claim to be particularly well versed in all this poetry flim-flam. I'm barely a passing fan. I've never had the kind of scholarly discipline that a deep appreciation for say, James Joyce, and I find Shakespeare downright excruciating.

I'm glad they're both dead.

Upon occasion, I've stumbled across poems that strike a chord, as long as I didn't have to work too hard to absorb them. Bukowski leaps to mind. I'm drawn to writers like Raymond Chandler, Richard Hell, Lennon, Pete Townsend, Ray Davies, Iggy Pop, Lou Reed, Nick Tosches, Dennis Johnson, Leonard Cohen, Dylan of course (although he's always pushing it), Jim Carroll, Hal David and Alice Cooper. It's all right up front for the taking — imagery, word-play, irony and cadence. It's real life played out in the streets.

It's guerilla warfare, and the weapons are words.

This is the poetic terrain on which I try to operate. Purists be damned. What qualifies as poetry anyway? Face it, you don't really know, do you? Hell, I don't either. Not so much as a clue. And I don't care either. I just call it rock and roll. Somehow, I'm more at peace with that. You can call it whatever you want. In the stories and lyrics that follow, I have made a concerted effort to lay them out in such a way that you will have a sense of both the beat and the spirit in which they were written. As some have said, (and I love hearing it), I write like a drummer; all blunt force trauma and rat-a-tat machine gun staccato bravado. It's out of my hands starting right now. You've been warned.

Keep the faith,

Rob McCuen
April 2015

1

GETTING BRAVE

I was a 6-year-old lab rat conducting an experiment on himself. This deal was life and death, and its outcome would determine all I would ever need to know about what I was made of. I had thrown down a challenge, and there could be no turning back. Yep, if a 6-year-old boy can have a vision, then I had one for the all-time ages. I was gonna be a racecar driver — the best who ever lived. I didn't quite have a handle on what it would take to get there, but my master plan was anything but chump change. I was gonna win the Indianapolis 500. And it was the time to get started.

I didn't know about the thousands of dollars it was gonna cost to launch my career, and I didn't know that kissing asses on the way to the top went with the territory, and I damn sure didn't understand the mechanical side of the sport. Mechanically, I didn't know a magneto from a monkey's ass, but I sure as hellfire knew about the brave. I knew that if I was gonna strap my skinny ass to 700 horsepower of supersonic widow-maker, I would need to be braver than Dick Dastardly. The time to prove it was now, the first defining moment of my young life.

So, there I stood, perched on the edge of my parents' picnic table, the peeling white paint curled up like toes, right there in my own backyard on a brilliant summer small town Iowa afternoon, psyching myself up for a true leap of faith. I think I was trying to talk to God, or maybe I was just talking to myself. There was no audience, nor did I require one. This was between me and my own soul.

I thought about my heroes, bad-ass armored warriors in tight white t-shirts and open-face helmets, chomping on cheap cigars and smirking right in the death dealer's face at 175 mph.

"If you're brave enough to be a racecar driver, then you better be brave enough to do a somersault off of this picnic table," said a tiny little voice inside of me. "Bobby Marshman, Parnelli Jones, A.J. Foyt and Jim Hurtubise are brave enough. What about you, boy?"

I must have stood there for a full ten minutes, steeling myself — just me, the green grass, the deep blue sky and that goddamn picnic table. Secretly, I wanted my mommy. I wasn't afraid of getting hurt, but I was terrified that I wouldn't have the guts to accept my own challenge. If I chicken-shitted out now, my life might as well be over. Mind you, I was only six. This stuff was for keeps.

I said a silent prayer and I was airborne. I stuck a perfect three-point landing, that is until my knees came up and smacked my chin with atomic force. I was stunned completely senseless, but even as I tasted the first wave of my own blood, the pain barely mattered, nor did having to get my tongue sewn back together. Nor did the severe concussion. I spent the night at Henry County Memorial. I got ice cream and sympathy.

Nothing, but nothing could dampen my spirits now. It was all in a day's work. I was a racecar driver — big and fast and brave.

2

TO CATCH A SERIAL KILLER

Gayno Smith had just shot, stabbed and bludgeoned just about his entire family to death. I was nine, staying with my paternal grandparents in Nothingsville, USA, also known as Sigourney, Iowa, when the news broke that a blood-lusting maniac was running rampant in our area. Gayno had always been known as a harmless, even gentle, man by those who knew him, a 24-year-old dullard who had been living with his aunt and uncle and their family of God-fearing farmers. There were six of 'em in all, and they were just simple folk, as were their needs. They farmed their 80 acres about four miles north of Martinsburg, a veritable hop, skip and jump south of Sigourney. They went to church, and they went to town for provisions. Maybe the odd ice cream social when they were in fun-seeking mode. Nobody ever had an unkind word to say about them.

In the spring of '62, for reasons that only God and Gayno will ever fully understand, Gayno Smith came unglued and took out five of the only people in the whole wide world who had ever shown him any kindness. The sixth got away after being shot in the shoulder and altered authorities, starting a manhunt. Little did anyone know at the time, but ole Gayno had taken out his stepmother the year before.

The papers and the TV said he was armed and dangerous and that there was a $5,000 reward for his dead or-alive capture. I was thrilled. Nothing ever happened in Sigourney, and good God did I hate that town. The only fun I ever had there was when my older cousin, Jon, would visit, and we would go to the salvage yard across the vacant lot and search for blood and chunks of smashed skulls on the dashboards of freshly wrecked cars. Apparently, the unruly delinquents from nearby Ottumwa got in fatal crack-ups pretty often. A little midday gore was the perfect preamble to Grandma McCuen's fried chicken dinners with homemade noodles.

Back in those days, when a TV bulletin interrupted regular programming, you could bet it was a big deal — not like nowadays, when every little item is breaking fucking news.

My ailing-from-emphysema grandfather owned a shotgun, but even I knew he was too sick to be any match for an off-the-deep-end fugitive like Gayno. The papers and TV said he was a mad man. Grandma was an imposing woman of sturdy German stock who could throw down world-class, made-from-scratch mincemeat pies. But she wasn't gonna be any help if Gayno showed up lusting for more blood. Her idea of a rocking Saturday night was knitting a sweater with her chronically arthritic hands while watching Billy Graham and

Lawrence Welk on their tiny 10-inch black and white.

So it all came down to me. I'd never even seen a gun before, but that wasn't gonna stop me. I decided to borrow Grandpa's 12-gauge and go looking for Gayno myself. It wasn't even about the money. Gayno was mean and evil, and I wanted him dead.

This was my first experience in life with sheer terror, and while I couldn't explain it at the time, I relished being in the clutches of absolute fear. It made me feel alive, a welcome reprieve from the daily drudgery of this shell of a town. The frequent, dramatic bulletins only added fuel to my fire. "GAYNO STILL AT LARGE. MAN-HUNT CONTINUES" screamed the headline.

I spent an entire day gathering weapons for my arsenal and hid them under the four-poster bed that my grandfather had so lovingly carved with his steady, ancient hands. If Gayno decided to come calling in the middle of the night, I had everything I would need to stop him in his cold-blooded killer tracks. As Grandma led me in my nighttime prayers, I couldn't wait for her to hit the hay so I could survey my inventory. I had a bag or oranges, a butcher knife, a Louisville slugger, a sackful of roofing nails and my ace in the hole, a pair of Grandpa's freshly sharpened (by me) golf cleats.

And of course, there was always that double barreled shotgun.

I lie awake all night, listening to the freight trains rumbling by a mere football field away. I was banking on Gayno being on one of those trains, and he was gonna get his, but good.

Sometime around sunup, I must've drifted off to sleep when suddenly I was startled awake by someone shaking me. A large, menacing figure was standing over me, mumbling incoherently.

"HOLY FUCK. IT'S GAYNO SMITH!"

Without hesitating, I reached under the blanket and whacked Gayno right between his slitted eyes with a golf shoe and followed it up with a shot to the back of his head with the bag or oranges. Gayno stumbled and fell with a dull thud and started to moan and whimper.

Turns out Gayno wasn't Gayno after all. It was Grandma, and she'd gotten up at the crack of dawn to make me homemade sugar doughnuts and mince-meat stew.

3

BROTHERS IN ARMS

They were brothers, but you really couldn't tell — just three meat and potatoes live-wire Midwestern boys with a zest for high livin'. They were all built real low to the ground, squat, barrel-chested and strong as a fleet of bulldozers. But still, there was little else to suggest that they shared the same bloodlines.

Circumstances that I was never privy to had separated them from their parents at birth, and whether by hook or crook, they were adopted by three families who just happened to live in the same neighborhood. By the time I met them, the boys were all but inseparable, and while local legend had it that they didn't know they were brothers, they were a roaming, roving, frothing-at-the-mouth power trio of piss and vinegar.

Whatever the force that bound them, they were a formidable presence in our town, and unless you were an idiot with a death wish, you tried your best to land on their good sides. The boys weren't mean so much as they were edgy, wound tight, and their code of ethics was a simple one — do unto others as they do to you, an eye for an eye, tit for tat and all that jazz. Treat 'em with the proper respect and all was well. Cross 'em and you had a fight on your hands.

Their names were Gus, Tony and Shaffner, whose real name was Barney, but you didn't dare ever call him that. He answered to "Shaffner," and he didn't need a reason. You called him "Shaffner" or ya didn't count. Not only was he the most cunning of the three, he was also the most predatory. He loved to hide in the bushes and lunge at unsuspecting passersby.

Paperboys especially appealed to him. His primary target for these blind-side bonsai assaults was a gangly, pigeon-toed oaf with orange hair and freckles named Marky Hammil. Although he probably never intended for these attacks to be vengeful, poor Marky became so unnerved, he developed a spastic twitch that resulted in his parents taking him to a specialist.

Eventually, Shaffner grew tired of attacking Marky, and they soon became thick as thieves, the best of friends. This became a pattern that he would repeat for as long as I knew Shaffner. He'd work his bully act until he had broken your spirit, then he'd turn on his considerable charm until you dropped your guard and became his lifelong chum. This was just Shaffner's way — a quirk — the way he chose his friends. Shaffner had a lot of friends.

One other thing about Barney that bears mentioning is that he just loved to eat. Lived for it, and his timing was impeccable. He knew exactly when everyone in town sat down to supper, and the way he had it figured, what better time for the old drop-in? All he had to do was show up and turn on the ole cutesy boy and viola, "chow time in carnivore city." His plan never failed him, and soon, he was mooching six, seven meals a night.

But not quite everybody relished Shaffner's presence and fell so readily for his boyish powers of persuasion. Shaffner wasn't about to let a little old thing like decorum cock block another free meal.

The McKims were a nice God-fearing family, and when Shaffner came around once too often, they even resorted to calling him "Barney the Beggar Boy" in a tactful, but futile, attempt to get him to quit coming around. The McKims simply didn't have it in them to tell their unwanted guest to just fuck the fuck off. Besides, they'd found themselves a nice little two-bedroom bungalow with a rec room and carport on over on the west side of town, and they figured that would be the last they'd ever see of Shaffner, the arrogant thug.

The McKims moved on the last weekend of November, and the following Tuesday, wouldn't ya know it? Shaffner had honed in on their new pad like a guided missile. Tuesday was pork chop night at the McKims' house, and Shaffner didn't give a shit if he had to trot across town for his favorite mooched meal. Shaffner lived for pork chops. Six-thirty sharp and there he was, wandering around the front yard with his favorite "feed me" expression, and brazenly, with more than a touch of "fuck you for trying to ditch me" attitude, this time he'd brought along his brother/pal, Gus.

Gus was an all-business motherfucker, level-headed and reserved by nature, but he commanded just as much respect as his brothers. He was a complete master of quiet intimidation. Gus knew how to get inside of your head, and he could pry you open like a can of rancid salmon. But recently, practically overnight, Gus had transformed into a vile beast, a crude bully who lacked both patience and honor. Worse yet, Gus was one of those creatures who had no restraint whatsoever when it came to his bodily functions. He burped, farted, puked and shit his way straight into the gross-out hall of fame, and the more he saw ya squirm, the deeper he'd reach into his bottomless bag of gut-churning parlor tricks.

Gus was losing friends by the dozen, but he didn't seem to care. Before long, even Tony and Shaffner snubbed him, and soon, Gus was left alone to revel in his low-brow kingdom. Just like that, Gus Krahl was a solo act, with only his brother, "Mole," to play with. Shaffner just acted like he couldn't be bothered by either one of them.

Tony still had a few other sidekicks around Shaeffer Addition, but after he stopped running with his brothers; he mostly just kept to himself. If he missed the old days, you sure couldn't tell it. He just went about his usual business. Tony was the high priest of cheap thrills, the scarier the better. His penchant for darting across streets into the paths of speeding cars became the stuff of legend. Every time we would hear screeching tires, angry horns and loud cursing, we would know that Tony had just dodged another bullet. Some of my friends were quick to write Tony off as a maniac, but I knew better. Risking his life was Tony's kick, his art, and he didn't give a god-hoppity-damn if he had an audience or not.

Soon, we became so captivated by Tony's daredevilry that we began to devise death-defying stunts just to see if we could get him to do 'em — and he nearly always would. One day, Fast Eddie Caldwell got the bright idea to pour gasoline on a hula-hoop, light it on fire and have Tony jump through a moving ring of fire. But the joke was on Fast Eddie this time. Eddie got careless with the gas and ended up with third-degree burns on his face and hands. Tony just snorted and ran away.

Two days later, Tony pulled his wildest stunt yet, jumping out of Butch Bentler's speeding pick-up truck on a whim. Tony, slid, flipped, skidded and tumbled for damn near 90 feet through Old Lady Shellebarger's immaculate garden before finally grinding to a violent halt. Tony laid there motionless for a moment, and we began to entertain the unthinkable horror that the stupid son-ovabitch was dead. Seconds later, Tony came to, shook his massive head from side to side, got up, and without so much as a whimper, tore off down the street like a just scalded pup.

Nobody saw him again for the rest of the week. We figured he was nursing his wounds and was too proud to let us see him hurt. I began to suspect that Tony was losing touch with reality. As the summer wore on, Tony began to push his luck to new heights, tempting fate every which way. He rarely even acknowledged me and the boys anymore. By mid-August, he was gimping around the neighborhood on a wounded leg that slowed everything but his non-stop quest for defying death.

"Tony, cool it will ya? You're gonna kill yourself one of these times!" I pleaded. But it was obvious that my appeal had failed to penetrate his extra-thick skull.

But Tony's salvation be damned. Let the fucker find out the hard way. I had something else on my mind for now. It was time once again for the Henry County Fair, even though it was a pathetic joke of a fair. There were more chickens and pigs than people. There were no freak shows and only six sad little kiddie rides. Even the carnies were lame. I wanted to see some child-hating serial killers running the Tilt-A-Whirl. Our carnies just looked hungover and defeated by life.

But the final Saturday night of the fair was the night we all lived for: RACE NIGHT! Our once mighty half-mile Iowa red clay oval had once been regarded as a major proving ground for some of racing's heaviest hitters. Parnelli Jones, Bobby Grim, the Daniels brothers "Scratch" and "Itch, Harold Leep, Greg Weld, Jerry Blundy, and even that old Texas bum, A.J. Foyt, had raced here. In 1957, my dad had seen a young lion named Red Hoyle perish in a crash so gory that the old man never went to another race as long as he lived. But the old joint had history and magic even if she was now nothing more than a worn out old horse track.

One night a year, she came back to life to give us a glimpse of her former glory. Hot damn, turn up the thrill-o-meter another 10,000 megatons, it's Saturday night and they're towing into Mt. Pleasant, Iowa, from all over the nation. Three hours before time trials, and my buddies and I were already perched high up in the glorious confines of that freshly, white-washed, Gothic-style grandstand. To hell with Tilt-A-Whirls and "Myrtle the Turtle Girl," heaven had taken the form of a half-mile of hallowed dirt heaven.

Dusk was in its final stages of panorama as they flagged 'em off for the trophy dash, a six-lapper featuring the six fastest qualifiers of the night. The track had risen to the occasion one more time and was deadly, wicked fast. The track record had been shattered three times during qualifying, and we were primed for a night of "THRILLS CHILLS and SPILLS," just like the four-color, day-glo posters promised.

As Tulsa's Buzzy Barton led the field out of Turn 4 and down the front chute, I saw him out of the corner of my eye. "HEY, IT'S TONY SMITH," I shouted. But no one could hear me over the high-pitched symphony of six maxed-out thoroughbred racing engines. "HE'S A GOOD FRIEND OF MINE."

Tony made a mad dash for the infield in plain view of 2,000 rednecks, farmers, greasers, geeks, punks, brats and motor heads. The grandstand reeked of Vitalis, cigarettes and burning rubber. Maybe Tony's gimp leg had thrown off his usual hair-trigger timing, but for whatever the reason, Barton hit him at full throttle and pitched Tony ten feet high into the multi-colored carnival sky. The crowd let out a collective gasp that was usually reserved for fires and roll-overs.

I was already on a dead run as the starter threw the red flag to halt the field. My sheer hysterics got me past the geezer at the pit gate, and I made it down to the race track just in time to watch Tony Smith die. He was in shock I'm sure, but I thought I saw a faint look of recognition in his eyes. He struggled to pull himself up, but it was obvious that he had broken his back. Tony stumbled and fell, his breathing reduced to a jagged hiss, like steam escaping from a broken pipe.

"Jesus Christ, Tony, get up, will ya?" I whispered through my tears.

There was one final twitch of his stubbly little mutt-dog tail as I stood there helplessly watching Tony Smith's soul sail straight off to doggie heaven, where the good doggies go.

4

OF MICE AND MYTHS

What kind of jerk would consider getting tossed out of Disneyland to be his finest hour? Well look no further my friends, for I am that jerk.

It was the summer of '64, the year the Beatles changed me forever. I was 11 years old, and my little sister, Mary, was eight, just the right age to make her the perfect foil for my constant emotional and physical torture. But Mary was no patsy, and she never, ever took my abuse lying down. She was a 44-pound whirling dervish, a kicking, scratching, biting, dump-truck-throwing ass kicker of the first degree. She used to wet her pants just to be contrary.

I had what you might call an adrenalin problem. Pre-Ritalin, pre-child harness, pre-politically correct and pre-behavioral disorders. Truth be told, I shoulda been in reform school. I guess I loved my kid sister as much as a punk like me could love his pain-in-the-ass sibling, but I'm here to tell ya, we were oil and water from day fucking one. "Spirited kids," they called us in the Sixties. These days, we woulda both been restrained.

But those were more innocent times. America was still buying into the Disneyland myth, and it was every kid's dream to go there. Mary and I were no exception, and with a little prodding, Dad sent away for the Mickey Mouse propaganda kit. Once the brochure arrived in the mail a week later, we were goners, and our excitement level was way over the moon. Mary liked the spinning cups and the jungle cruise. The Matterhorn made my eyeballs spin, that is until I saw the ultimate attraction for an aspiring young racer like me — an exact quarter-scale replica of the LA Freeway, complete with single-seat, convertible, open cockpit sports cars.

Man of action that dad was, he jelled the vacation plans in a matter of an afternoon. Given the family history of disharmony while driving, we decided to fly to California. My mother, ever the culture buff, wanted to stop at every museum within 200 miles. She was always voted down. I liked caves, reptile gardens, Indian ceremonials and motel swimming pools with three-meter diving boards. Mary just wanted to go anywhere that she could order Shrimp Louie.

Then there was dad, never the champion of chill, hell-bent on whatever destination he had crammed into his built-in sense of extreme urgency. The last thing you were ever gonna hear from my dad was, "Aw gee kids, let's just point the Mercury west today and see where we end up." It was more like, "Get in the goddamn car already, we gotta make Idaho by sunset."

All the while, my mother, ever the world's most alert co-pilot, was always warning dad about the semi truck with its turn blinker on a mile up the highway. This usually meant war. So any damn way you sliced it, flying to California was a simple act of family preservation.

I bought the hype surrounding the plane ride until the second we boarded. Just when it started to get good, it was over. So boring. "Don't rip the magazines." "Stop pulling your sister's pigtails." "Don't get out of your seat." "Stop putting gum in your sister's hair!"

Great balls of Moses, I thought we'd never land. We were cruising at more than 500 mph, but there was zero sensation of speed. The whole trip sucked. All I wanted to do was strap into that shiny red sports car and cause a 17-car pile-up on the LA Freeway.

Mom and Dad stuck to us like tension headaches on our first day at Disneyland. I guess I had about as much fun as an 11-year-old could have when his parents were hawkeying his every move. We did about everything a kid could do in one day, except for the exalted LA Freeway ride, which had a line all the way to Mexico from the looks of it. My father knew what this attraction meant to me, and he promised that we'd hit the park extra early the next day. With that, we went back to the Mouse Motel, and Mary ordered Shrimp Louie.

I tossed and turned all night in anticipation of that ride. I was gonna race tomorrow, I was really gonna race. Needles on the dash quivered and spun until my mind veered from the LA Freeway to the Indianapolis Motor Speedway and "the greatest spectacle in racing."

My racing fantasies ran amok. I wasn't in a toy sports car anymore, I was in a sleek Offy roadster built by the god of all racecar builders, A.J. Watson. I'd be starting in the ninth row, so I knew I was really gonna have to stand on the loud pedal. Still, I just knew that I was gonna win, an 11-year-old boy wonder prodigy from small-town Iowa kissing the 500 Queen and hoisting the Borg-Warner trophy up high and proud. This time tomorrow, I'd be a fucking legend.

Race day dawned cool and clear, a beautiful day for racing. Mom and Dad walked Mary and me to the gate and sealed the authenticity of my fantasies with the most golden words ever spoken: "Rob, I want you to keep an eye on your little sister today. Your mother and I are going to catch a show at the GE Carousel. Here's $150 worth of tickets. Have fun and be careful!"

This was my cue. I grabbed Mary by the scruff of her neck and began dragging her toward the race track, ignoring her squeals of protest. By 9:30, I was at the drivers meeting, and by 10, I was being buckled in by my "crew."

"Good luck, boy, don't kill yourself," muttered my crew chief, Clint Brawner. By now, I could almost hear Jim Nabors singing, "Back Home Again in Indiana."

My sister was one row ahead of me, but she wasn't my sister anymore, she was the great Eddie Sachs, the clown prince of racing, in the Dean Van Lines Special, just one of the 26 cars I was gonna hafta pass to get to the front.

"No problem," I smirked to myself cockily, "I'll have these slow-motion pigeons eating out of my hand."

But suddenly, there was a hitch, and not a small one. The brochures hadn't shown this, but there was a metal rail running through the center of the track, no doubt designed with kids like me in mind. You were driving, but only sort of. As soon as you veered too far in either direction, the wheels would strike the rail and straighten you back out. This made passing impossible.

Or did it?

By the time we entered Turn 2, I was committed. I figured if I gave Sachs/Mary a hard shot in the rear left-side quarter panel at just the proper angle as she approached the corner, I could bang her off the track and get past her.

My evil plan worked only too well.

I timed the hit perfectly, and I thrilled at the sight of her wildly spinning roadster as it jumped the track and plummeted 25 feet down an embankment, landing upside down in a ravine and ejecting my sister from the twisted wreckage.

"Cool, only 25 more cars to pass," I snickered to myself. I could hear Sachs/Mary whimpering from her crumpled racer. I didn't have time to worry about my mortally wounded sister, I was already setting up my next victim, Lloyd Ruby, I think it was.

And that's when the curtains came crashing down hard on my Indy 500 fantasies. I could really have used a helmet at this point. I was swarmed by hordes of Disney henchmen in orange Mickey Mouse jumpsuits, and they appeared to be more than a little pissed. Bewildered and still in racing mode, it took me a few moments to realize that I was the object of their wrath. One of the bigger Mickey hitmen dragged me outta the cockpit by my Dennis Wilson bangs and started slappin' me around.

"Hey kid, who the fuck you think you are? A.J. Foyt or something?"

With that, I was unceremoniously ejected from the park. I think they woulda beat me, too, but they were probably bound by the Mickey Mouse oath not to strike children. This was Disneyland, for Chrissakes. How would it look?

I was inconsolable, but only momentarily. I mean, how was I to blame that their little kiddie track couldn't contain my need for speed? Fuck their rules and their little toy kiddie cars. I had again exceeded limits and shattered track records.

Disneyland was now just one more lousy memory. Who needed it? I was a kid, and an "about face" was business as usual. I went back to my world of GI Joe on the front lines, Barbie and Ken gettin' their freak on in the beach house, the Black Panthers, the Beatles, trick race cars, girls in see-through bikinis, Tiger Beat Magazine, the Smothers Brothers, napalm and miniskirts. Back to a world that was building bomb shelters and bracing for World War III, racing toward the moon.

5

A FEW WORDS ABOUT MY MOTHER

Whenever I wanna channel my dead mother, I clean. Doesn't even matter what — I scrub, sweep, dust and polish. My mother couldn't help herself — she cleaned that sprawling four-bedroom, two-and-a-half-bath, ranch style home with an eight-foot, slate-bed Brunswick pool table and rec room down in the basement from morning until night. And the woman always looked like June Cleaver while doing it. Okay, so maybe she wasn't draped in pearls, but she might as well have been.

Mother was a coffee achiever, and she never seemed to run out of juice. I used to wonder if she didn't have a hidden stash of benzedrine socked away somewhere in her meticulous kitchen cabinets. Just to give you some perspective on the degree of my mom's cleaning fetish, try this on for size: In 2004, when she was 74 years old, she had a third of her cancerous right lung removed. Three days after being released from hospital, she was down on her hands and knees scrubbing the kitchen floor, somehow looking stylish and elegant all the while.

Matter of fact, some called her "Elegant Alice." Others called her "the Jackie O. of Mt. Pleasant, Iowa." And she was. With my father ever the big man around town, mother was forced into the role of first lady. She hated it, but she always shined. In the 1960s, first ladies weren't allowed the luxury of not being "on."

Yep, she was a class act through and through, and one of my most lasting and precious images of her was when she'd had one too many glasses of Chablis. Her little hands would get to fluttering, and that endearing half-suppressed giggle of hers would become a bit more animated. Somehow, she even made being drunk look lady-like. Just to give you some idea of the degree of beauty we're talking about here, in 1947, my mother was voted "America's Most Beautiful Teenager."

And oh, one of the judges was Cary Grant.

She was also the homecoming queen at Oskaloosa High School and later at Iowa Wesleyan College, where she met my father as an ultra-feminine, frightened, insecure little freshman majoring in home economics, a sign of the times. Women then were little more than arm candy and symbols of virility. Two years later, she was crowned Queen of the Drake Relays. Her beauty never once went to her head, and she was always kind and considerate to everyone she ever met. Nobody, but nobody didn't love her. She had more friends than anybody I've ever known.

Where our relationship was concerned, mother was torn. She didn't approve of my irreverent and often mean-spirited wit, but in spite of her obsession with always being prim and proper, she secretly found me hysterical. Whenever I would say something outrageous or obnoxious, or over the top, which was daily, mom would cover her mouth with those tiny, sculpted hands to stifle her laughter and say, "OH, ROB," in mock disgust. She laughed in spite of herself, and I lived for that. My mother often didn't approve of me, but one thing's for certain — she got me like no one else ever has.

Her home was her pride and joy, and sadly, as the years went by, she became more and more of a slave to it. She was always too busy scrubbing stuff to accept the many invitations from friends who tried in vain to get her away from that goddamn house. Even her illness couldn't slow her down, and when the cancer progressed to the terminal stage, I learned one more thing about my mama. I had always thought that racecar drivers (and NO, I don't mean NASCAR) were the bravest sonsa-bitches on the planet until I had to so helplessly watch my mother dying. No one has ever died with more grace, dignity or bravery. She was as tough as she was precious.

Even in her final days, her home, her family, and her friends were her pride and joy, and even after my father left her after 35 years of marriage for a money grubbing, inbred, hybrid hillbilly whore from southern Missouri, she never stopped redesigning the interior of her personal showcase palace. Through all the changes, it always felt like home.

On Oct. 5, 2007, at the age of 77, mother finally succumbed to her illness, her once shapely figure now reduced to a ravaged 80 pounds of bare bones.. I'm not a particularly religious man, but if there's a heaven up there somewhere, it was surely made just for Alice Jean Barnes-McCuen.

6

ROASTING MY FATHER OVER AN OPEN FIRE

My dad was always a busy guy, ambitious as all hell. He was president of this and chairman of that. Growing up, it seemed like my father was in charge of damn near everything. One thing that really stands out — no matter where he was going or what he was doing — he was always the first one there and the first one to leave. I never saw a checkered flag at the races or heard a final gun at a ballgame until I was old enough to grow up and move away. I never did learn the source of his intense urgency, but I think it had something to do with beating the traffic. My father hated traffic.

Everything, and I mean everything, was done at the speed of sound. Take our first fishing trip for example. My first cast of the day was a complete disaster, and I got the line hung up in a sickly old maple tree. Dad tried to finesse the line loose for about ten minutes, a lifetime for him, and when that failed, he resorted to hissing profanities under his breath, and then brute force.

Nothing doing. The line was hopelessly tangled and out came Dad's trusty pocket knife. He cut it loose and unceremoniously announced that we were all done fishing.

Our next bonding ritual revolved around the game of golf, but not by any means, golf in the conventional sense. When I was around six, my mom put her foot down and demanded that my father start spending more time with his only son.

Now Dad was fine with this mandate, but damned if he was gonna let his golf game suffer for it. This would prove to be the beginning of a father-and-son rite of passage that I would come to cherish above all else. Dad would lovingly order me to lie down on my back and not move a muscle. He'd spend the next two hours teeing up Titleists off of my forehead and blasting away with his driver. Dad was always a pretty crummy golfer and I took my fair share of violent shots to the skull.

I never questioned it — I thought this was what fathers and sons did together. I didn't yet know the difference between quality time and child abuse. Actually, I came to relish these lazy Saturday mornings of blood, booze and hallucinations. In his infinite wisdom, Dad discovered that if he fed me two or three shots of Jim Beam, not only did I become a more stable human golf tee, I could also withstand a butt load more pain.

But it was the days that dad decided to work on his short game that I came to dread the most. A direct hit to the temple with a driver was one thing — a sand wedge to the cheekbone is a whole other animal. My dad couldn't chip to save his ass, and I took a savage beating.

Loving and thoughtful father that he was, though — after ripping out huge chunks of flesh from my face, dad never once failed to replace the divots. Then, knocked unconscious, he would take my lifeless body to the A&W for root beer and French fries. And that's when I knew for sure — my dad really did love me.

7

THE FIRST CUT IS THE DEEPEST

Catholic chicks — holy Christ good God almighty! While they were busy praying, I got busy preying on that notorious Catholic guilt, and lemme tell ya straight up — it ain't no myth. The Jews may have invented the concept of guilt, but Catholics took it to a whole other level. As a self-proclaimed prophet once told me while in the grips of a three day whiskey-bender at the Uptowner (and boy what a place to acquire wisdom that down-and-out joint is), "Jews feel guilty about letting down their mothers while the Catholics only worry about disappointing God."

The trouble with damn near every Catholic girl I've ever dated is that they really like sex. And I mean a lot. Why would that be a problem you say? Well, sooner than later, that goddamn Catholic guilt kicks in and they send you so many mixed signals you'd swear that you'd spent your night in a cement mixer. I think maybe it's bred into their DNA or something.

My first serious girlfriend was a raging Cathoholic from Dutch descent and, oh my God, what a blonde, blue-eyed bombshell of a teenage beauty she was — a real show stopper. Imagine Tuesday Weld at 15, and you're in the ballpark. How she ended up with me I'll never know. When you factor in my 17-year-old love/lust to the mix, no lie, this tiny 103-pound sex kitten had me foaming at the mouth like a rabid wolf-hound. She kept me so goddamned tweaked out, I almost converted just to get in her panties sooner.

I knew right away I was in way over my head, but at that age, it's a blowout — your hormones always win. Believe me when I tell ya, being in love with Katie Van Tiger was like wading into a gang fight with a pencil.

I probably should have married the vivacious little vixen, but I wasn't the marrying kind. Matter of fact, I'm still not. So when I packed off to Truman State University to major in drugs, racing, rock and roll and girls, it didn't take Katie long to find a more stable and suitable replacement — honor student, son of a college history professor, Hitler youth handsome and conference champ varsity wrestler. Well, junior varsity, but still. Katie and Kurt, 'til death do them part. He was such an all-around good guy I couldn't even muster up any hatred for the bastard. Now semi-retired, he and Katie recently bought a small farm outside of Omaha with their four perfect children. I wish I could say I'm happy for them, but I'm not.

In the summer of 2006, stuck in my hometown while helplessly watching my mother withering away from cancer, I would compulsively drive past Katie's old house on East Warren every damn day, fixating wistfully at her second-story bedroom window, even though she hadn't lived there for almost

30 years. One lost night, drinking at the only bar in town that served Maker's Mark bourbon, I managed to procure her phone number from a mutual friend and cold-called her right out of the blue.

She sounded exactly the same — a voice like velvet and that low, throaty purr of a laugh of hers. I loved her still. I somehow resisted the urge to go all mushy and nostalgic.

I almost worked up the nerve to ask her if she ever thought about those coming-of-age sessions of heavy petting and hot kisses out on County Road K, but I'd bet my Mt. Pleasant Panther football jersey (#3) that she does. I know I sure as fuck do. We even had a regular Friday night sex routine: Unless I had a ballgame, I'd pick Katie up at 7:30 sharp and we'd head 23 miles straight north on U.S. Highway 218 to Ernie's Tap in Crabwell Corners and get trashed on whatever putrid swill Ernie was trying to unload from his already pathetic inventory. At 40 cents a draw, we could get wasted on like eight bucks. Ole Ernie's serving policy was a simple one — if you had some dough in your jeans and could see over the bar, you were golden. You could be 12, Ernie didn't care. Better still, he never once cut us off.

I had to be home at 11:30 senior year cuz I was on probation for robbing a corner grocery, a caper that went wrong from the start. One day, right before the big game with the much hated Oskaloosa Indians, the cops showed up at practice and hauled my ass away. I said I didn't do it, but it was no use; they had me cold.

The jig was up. No football and no fun for poor Robbie. As a consequence, Katie and I were always racing the clock. It ain't easy to get drunk and laid in just four hours, especially when you subtract the 45-minute round-trip drive time. Our mobile motel was my mom's cherry 289 V8 '67 Mustang convertible with bucket seats and an ultra-obtrusive automatic T-shifter stuck right there between us. The space limitations were annoying as all hell, but we were like a couple of circus contortionists. On the rare occasion when I could con my old man into forking over the keys to his Electra 225, we always felt like we had a luxury suite at the downtown Des Moines Hilton.

After slamming back one more for the road, it quickly became time to get serious. Speeds to our private little pit of passion were generally in the 90-110 mph range. Mustangs of that era had seriously twitchy handling characteristics once you got them up over 80, and drunk as I always was, I can't believe I didn't kill us both. The only thing that saved us was my arrogance. I steadfastly believed that I was a racecar driver just cuz I had won some go-kart races. Poor Katie would turn ghostly white with fear, but for me, high-speed danger and sex were practically the same thing. There never seemed to be any cops around, and besides, driving drunk in the '70's was like a badge of honor. Almost nobody ever got popped.

As the kisses got hotter and the windows got steamier, my roving hands were like an octopus. Katie had recently been groped during a photo op with that old pervert Col. Sanders, and it occurred to me through my drunken haze that the Colonel must've found Katie to be about as finger-lickin' good as I did. Katie might have been a good little Catholic girl, but the lust and the booze seemed to trump her guilt every time. Only then were we free to succumb to the taboo temptations of Christ.

The very next afternoon, there I'd be, faithfully sitting on the steps of St. Alphonsus Church, chain smoking stale Pall Malls, while my sweet Katie was

inside spilling her guts to some half-drunk priest who was probably fantasizing that she was a he.

But what the fuck did I care? I was raised Presbyterian, and as near as I could tell, we didn't stand for a goddamn thing. Soon, Katie would emerge, looking all radiant and refreshed, her spirit now cleansed by Christ and a couple of hundred Hail Marys. Cool. Now we were golden to sin all over again. Guilt-free. And so we did. Over and over again.

Amen.

8

AN EVENING TO KILL IN MISSOURI

So, there I was sitting in some faceless prefab motel room in Springfield, Missouri, thinking about how to kill an evening. I'd just driven 600 miles in just under ten hours, and I should be tired, but I'm not. I'm jacked up on truck stop coffee and a brush with vehicular manslaughter, where some idiot in a semi hauling port-o-potties suddenly drifted into my lane while I was doing 75 mph on a sweeping left-hander on I-44. I didn't have time to see my life flash before my eyes or any of that new-age hokum, but I'll tell ya this much — I was about a foot away from being a grease spot. Death by shit wagon. Excellent.

"Seinfeld" is on in ten minutes. That'll kill half an hour, but then what?

I used to live in Missouri so I have no illusions. It's gonna be a long fucking night.

I'm in the heart of the Ozarks, one of America's original low budget sucker traps; it's Missouri's answer to the Wisconsin Dells. It preys on the fat, the lazy, and the easily amused, the same kind of sweatpants around-the-clock losers who shop at Walmart. They've got a cave down here where you don't even have to walk; they just stuff you into the back of a Jeep like a bunch of propped-up cadavers, and away you go. And you won't wanna miss the roadside "Exotic Animal Ranch," either. Again, walking is not an option. Somehow, observing wild animals in what is advertised as "a natural setting" seems to lose some of its charm when you're forced to remain in your car, doncha reckon?

If it wasn't the dead of winter, I could have gone fishing at Lake Rube-a-doo, the world's largest bass lake. I find it hysterical that they've managed to work the word "rube" into the name of this aquatic clip joint. I'm banking on the management having a sense of humor, but it's just as likely merely a happy accident. Nobody's that clever down here. I can only assume that fishermen must also do their fishing without ever leaving the comfort of their own automobiles.

But so much for lost tourist opportunities. I glance out the window, and it appears that the cocktail lounge at the neighborhood Applebee's is by far my best option, though I also take note of a gaudy neon sign that promises "A GENUINE HILLBILLY BREAKFAST" for $3.99. Now I'm as big of a sucker as the next guy when a grease-soaked cholesterol fest is only a stone's throw away, but I reckon the country bumpkin vibe is gonna be competing for a mighty heapin' helpin' of my attention with the K-Mart right down yonder.

Christ! This is bleak. "Seinfeld" has come and gone, and in keeping with my general state of agitation, I've seen this episode once too often. It's the one where Jack Klompus gives Jerry his astronaut pen, the one that writes upside down. George and Kramer were bitchslapped right outta the script. It's weak, and another harsh reminder of how fragile the psyche can be when you're alone in a motel room and a slave to what's on television.

No wonder people kill themselves in settings such as these.

Morbidly, I scan the carpet and walls for blood stains, but see no verifiable signs of murder or suicide. There is, however, a hastily patched-over hole in the bathroom wall that is just the right size to have had a human skull shoved clean through it. But this is probably just wishful thinking on my part. Sick though it is, I'd somehow feel better spending the night in this soul-sucking, thirty-three-dollar-a-night prison cell if I thought it had some violent history. Or any history.

I get a renewed sense of hope when I notice a bullet-sized hole in the ceiling above my bed. Excitedly, I jump up and probe the hole for powder burns, but all I get for my trouble is an eyeball full of insulation.

I'm a dime store detective without a crime to solve.

What passes for a ceiling is nothing more than three-eighths-inch drywall covered with a stucco style imitation plaster. It's too flimsy to withstand a speeding bullet without collapsing completely. Disappointed, I figure that it's likely nothing more than a cork from a bottle of Cold Duck or some equally repulsive cut-rate drug store champagne, but I take strange solace from conjuring up images of the ultimate hayseed honeymoon right here in room number 103 of this God-forsaken, bible-belt budgetel.

I decide I'm tired of being Sam Spade.

It's time to determine whether Applebee's "something good in the neighborhood" really is anything more than just an idle threat. Immediately, the bartender bristles at my order. She's never heard of Maker's Mark. I resign to lower my standards and order a Jim Beam on the rocks. As my week progressed, I learned that nobody in either Missouri or Oklahoma knows how to pour a good, stiff drink. Back home in Milwaukee, I actually have to tell the goddamn liquor pushers to back the fuck off. Trust me, If you dare to enter a bar in Milwaukee, you better make peace with this pardner; you're gonna leave smashed.

It takes about 30 seconds to size the joint up. Whatever it is I think I'm looking for, I'm not gonna find it here. I slam my $5 kiddie cocktail in a single, mighty gulp and summon the bartender.

"Yeah, where can I see some live music around here?"

She looks at me like I've got a scrotum growing out of my forehead. "On a Tuesday night? You must be joking. This is the bible belt, sir."

Trying not to sound as desperate as I felt, I press her for an entertainment tip."Yeah, but there must be something to do around here."

She perks up immediately and says, "Hey, wait a minute, I know. You could still make the 8 o'clock show over at Branson."

For those of you who may not know, Branson is where the stars who are too washed up for even game shows or side rooms in Reno go to die. It's the only venue left in Amerikkka where the audience is as doomed as the performers.

It's the end of the line.

Morbid motherfucker that I am, I feel a flicker of hope. I revel in watching once great singers and comedians trying to get it up one last time after their chops have been sucked dry by time.

"Fuckin' A," I practically scream, "who's playin'?"

"Steve Lawrence and Shecky Green," she chirps, grateful to suddenly find herself thrust into the role of entertainment director. "My grandmother saw the show on New Year's Eve and she can't stop talking about it. Says it was the best show she ever saw except for Perry Como right before he died."

I think to myself, "how can you tell if Perry Como is alive or dead in the first place?" The motherfucker was about the most relaxed performer who ever lived. When compared to Perry Como, Dean Martin was Iggy Pop in the live-wire department.

I weighed my options, and suddenly, contemplating suicide in a lonesome fleabag motel seemed like a pretty goddamn viable way to kill an evening after all.

A mere 30 minutes away, Steve Lawrence is probably serenading the blue-haired incontinents with a rollicking rendition of "Chestnuts Roasting on an Open Fire." And people say being alone in a motel room is depressing.

I swelled with a newfound sense of well-being. Hells bells, Hoss, I've got everything to live for. When I wake up tomorrow morning, I'm fixin' to get me a genuine hillbilly breakfast buffet down the road a spell.

Tonight Springfield, Missouri. Tomorrow the world!

9

BECAUSE YOU KNOW ME

They were calling it the worst blizzard in 65 years, and to make matters worse, it was 23 below zero. Everything in Champaign, Illinois, was either canceled or closed.

"Stay home, it's treacherous out there. Under no circumstances should anybody venture outside for any reason," said John Ravencraft, Champaign/Urbana's most trusted and dependable TV anchor, in his most earnest TV anchor voice.

I couldn't believe my extraordinary good fortune. I was snowbound with a raven-haired Jewish beauty named Veronica Stein and her twin sister, Victoria. My sexual fantasies ran amok as I ran down the possibilities that this act of a kind, just God had afforded me. I had almost everything a man could need under circumstances such as these. We had a case and a half of Falstaff, a pint of gin, eight grams of Panama Red weed, a quart of Rebel Yell, and for good measure, just over a gram of blonde, Lebanese hashish.

The twins had a respectable — though hardly what you would call spectacular — record collection, but they owned enough Aerosmith, Cheap Trick, the Who and Skynard records to keep a good edge going for at least a couple of days.

"I wonder if they have a Twister game," I recall thinking from the pornographic recesses of my mind. But there was one problem and not a small one.

I was almost out of cigarettes.

"We're going out, I need smokes," I announced abruptly.

"Oh don't talk crazy. You heard John Ravencraft. We can't go out in this. I've got some Kent filters my mom left here at Thanksgiving," said Veronica.

"Get your coat, baby, I smoke Marlboros," I said stubbornly. "C'mon, it will be an adventure."

"Why do I know I'm going to live to regret this?" countered Veronica with a nervous shriek of a laugh.

"Because you know me," I snickered.

"You guys are idiots," I heard Victoria say from the kitchen as we headed for my conversion van.

I wasted no time in demonstrating my Hollywood stuntman driving prowess. Controlled power-slides and 360-degree spin outs were second nature. There was no one else on the road.

"Jesus Christ, this is spooky. It's like the apocalypse out here. Nothing is going to be open, fuckhead. Look, even Van's Tap is shut down. I got some sweet sugar for ya baby, if you just turn around and take me home. It's awful out here," whispered Veronica weakly. "Are cigarettes really that important to you?"

"Relax, " I sneered as I snuffed the life out of my next-to-last smoke. "There's a 24-hour truck stop out on North Mattis Avenue."

I mashed the gas to the floor to emphasize my point, countersteering with the deft touch of Parnelli Jones as the back end swung around in search of some bite. It was a routine slide job — no big deal — but I had underestimated the severity of the conditions. I almost saved her, but when my left rear wheel kissed the shoulder, four feet of virgin snow sucked me axle deep into the ditch.

"ALL RIGHT HOLD TIGHT I'M A HIGHWAY STAR." This Deep Purple number was an anthem for every street racing kid in America, but now, as it blared through my tricked-out, three-way Jensen speakers, it sounded like a taunt. Veronica sealed the moment: "Nice going, dickhead! Now what is your dumb ass gonna do?"

I lit my last cigarette. "Not another fucking word, "I snapped through clenched teeth.

It didn't take long for the situation to reach the critical stage. This was still my fashion period, and I considered dressing for the weather to be a weakness of character. You live by the sword, you better be ready to die by the fucker. I was decked out in low-cut purple corduroy bell-bottoms, Beatle boots with four-inch Cuban heels, a yellow leather jacket with no lining and a broken zipper … and for good fashion measure, a multicolored ascot. I was freezing to death, and Veronica, resplendent in a black cocktail dress and a mink stole, but with at least some regard for the elements, wasn't faring much better.

In a nutshell, we were double-clutch fucked.

"I'm going for help. You coming or do ya wanna wait in the van?" I said impatiently.

"Oh dear God," whimpered my unwilling partner in cheap, tawdry thrills. "We're gonna freeze to death for sure and all because of your stupid cigarettes."

"You need to just shut the fuck up," I said testily. "Here's the news. We ain't got a whole lot of time to kick around options. We're almost out of gas."

With that, Veronica turned white as the driven snow. "Okay, I'll go with you, I guess," she said without conviction, "but I want you to know that this is easily the worst date of my life. You are such an idiot!"

As the first light of day began to crack over the flat, Illinois horizon, we started walking in the general direction of a prefab neighborhood about a mile away. We had no master plan, and freezing to death soon became a real possibility. Veronica was whimpering and whining non-stop, which only made me angrier than I already was. Didn't she understand? I was a racecar driver, and crashing was never an option. This clearly hadn't been my fault. Of course, this wasn't the first time my race driver fantasies had gotten me into deep shit. But never axle deep.

A half an hour later, we came upon a welcome sight, an oasis in the midst of this mid-winter torture chamber. I spotted a garbage truck idling in the driveway outside of a cheap-looking, two-bedroom home. The house was painted a sickly yellow with lime green trim. Offended sensibilities aside, we needed help, and we needed it now. Frostbite had already invaded my face and feet, and Veronica was claiming that she couldn't feel her legs.

Clearly, we were in real trouble.

I knocked loudly at the door for a full three minutes before the door flew open, suddenly and violently. An oversized Doberman leaped at the door, hitting it so hard that the screen gave in a full foot and almost tore loose from the frame. When I had recovered from the shock of this near brush with a gnarly death, I glanced up, and what do I see? A 12-gauge shotgun trained right on my frostbitten face. Veronica let fly with a blood-curdling scream, and the shotgun moved point blank to her right temple.

"What the fuck do you fuckers want? I gotta get to work," demanded the man.

Gathering myself up enough to at least get a sentence out, I said, "Can we please come inside? I crashed my van in a snowdrift on Mattis Avenue, and we're freezing to death."

"What are ya, fucking stupid? Nobody should be out in this shit. Didn't you hear Ravencraft? I gotta work, but what the fuck's your excuse?"

"I needed cigarettes," I answered.

Somehow, my explanation seemed to soften the man, but only slightly. "I can relate, motherfucker. Come on in."

We gratefully entered and sat down on a torn, overstuffed sofa. There was porn, spent shotgun shells and gun magazines all over the floor. A large swastika flag was displayed over the second-hand television and a second flag that served as a curtain said "WHITE POWER." Not lost on me was the fact that the shotgun was still aimed straight at our heads. "So if you need to make a call, you better fucking make it, "warned the man. I ain't got all motherfuckin' day."

I dialed Beasley's Cab Service and was told that the wait would be at least an hour. "Okay, I guess," I said, my heart sinking.

"It's gonna be at least an hour," I told the man. I was beginning to feel like a hostage."

"I'll tell ya what, fuck face. You gimme 20 bucks and I'll take you and your little whore to the cabstand.

"Deal!" I said, more than willing to sell out Veronica's honor. "Can we stop for cigarettes?"

"Don't press your luck, boy." answered Mr. Angry. "My name is Teddy. Ya got the 20 on ya?" I assured him that I did and forked over the cash. "You wanna throw in the broad?" Teddy said creepily.

We got in the garbage truck, and wouldn't ya know it, Teddy kept the shotgun right there on his lap all the way to the cabstand. He dropped us off with a final pearl of wisdom: "Hey, you fuckers should come over tonight. Drink some fuckin' beer. Watch some fuckin' porn. I got a shooting range in my basement. How 'bout it? Actually, YOU can stay home, faggot," he said pointing at me, "I'm more interested in your hot little bitch."

"No thanks, Teddy. Veronica and I are getting married tonight," I proclaimed.

"Fuck you both then," snarled Teddy.

We waited at the cabstand for an hour and a half, me angry, cold and jonesing bad for a cigarette. Veronica wasn't talking to me or anybody. My raven-haired knockout turned frigid monster just sat there crying and shivering. Finally, she gives me a rough poke in the chest and says, "Listen. You aren't getting ANY of this sweet sugar. My sister and I both wanted to do you, but you blew that, you fucking lunatic. We were even gonna break out our Twister game. We had big plans for you until you tried to kill me. So, here's the fucking deal — when we get back to my house, I'm going straight to bed, and when I wake up, your dumb ass better be gone."

"But what am I supposed to do? Where am I supposed to go?" I asked weakly.

Veronica stiffened. "You better call your buddy, Teddy, why doncha? Now get the fuck outta my sight!"

10

JUMBO JETS AND CIGARETTES

I love cigarettes so much, I'm willing to die for them. Allow me to explain.

I have no idea what the Kuwaiti populace is drawn to. I do know that their work week runs Saturday through Wednesday, and I think I have a pretty firm grasp on what they eat and the God they by-and-large embrace. And I know, too, that they have more oil than Vegas has peep shows. Also, beneath their ridiculous cloaks, they have more than their fair share of beautiful women — women who have rubbed themselves against the fabric of so-called Western-world sophistication.

And I know one more thing: Their airline might as well be run by the Keystone Kops. The planes are cold, drafty and hopelessly outdated. Maintenance? Minimal at best. Nothing works. The toilets don't flush, my footrest is sheared off at the base and you can forget about watching a movie — the electric motor that drives the screen doesn't engage. There are no headphones, and the closest thing to music is the non-stop wailing of over a dozen babies as they gulp for air through the purple-poison haze of 63 rows of chain smoking nicotine freaks.

My flight was scheduled to depart Chicago at 7:15 in the morning, and like a sucker, I arrived two hours early, as advised. At least I had the good sense to call ahead, and I was assured that Flight 116 non-stop to Amsterdam was right on time. At exactly 7:45, we were instructed to board for takeoff. I figure that any time you're stuck with flying out of the daily debacle that is O'Hare International, anything less than a two-hour delay is a moral victory.

Killer kind bud, a rich daddy, the love of my life (or so I thought at the time) and ten glorious days of pure European decadence was only an ocean away.

We take our seats, and within moments, one of the battalion of baby brats right across the aisle from me burps up a lap full of gross-out goo that looks like something between bile and a liquefied Hershey bar all over his mother's white terry cloth pants suit. She's the world's most ill-prepared mother. She's got no towels, no baby wipes, not so much as a lousy tissue, and now, she starts calling her bouncing baby boy names like "stupid little shithead" and "worthless bastard," and airline personnel is like nowhere to be found, like vanished.

By now, some of the passengers are gagging and puking, too, and the fucking baby is screaming like he's been dipped in boiling oil, and still no sign of the crew in sight. There's a man with ping pong-sized growths all over his face sitting in the very rear corner of the plane trying to stay invisible until finally, reluctantly, when he can't take another second of the shrieking and the piercing stench, he struggles to his feet and tries to hand a tissue to the near-hysterical mother. She recoils in horror and yelps with a voice that sounds like lug nuts in a blender: "You can keep your disease-ridden tissues, you filthy leper! Can somebody help me here?"

The man, this poor, deformed, frightened sweet soul of a man who makes the Elephant Man look like Paul Newman at his most dashing and was just trying to help, slinks back to his seat shamefully and tries to cover up his face with hands that resemble shriveled bacon. Finally, a prim flight attendant with a Cleopatra haircut and an undisguised expression of disgust emerges from her hiding place and tosses a soggy towel in the general direction of the mayhem. Wordlessly, she sneers and disappears again.

Two hours crawl by.

No music, no explanations, not even so much as a crummy cocktail as a filled-to-capacity jetliner perches on the tarmac like a wounded, prehistoric bird. Outside, the thermometer hovers at 25 below. At long last, a catering truck wheels up to the rear hatch, and the door swings wide open. Arctic air rushes along the fuselage, and three flight attendants scurry up the aisle like flaming cockroaches, seeking warmth. A small army of expressionless personnel begin their maneuvers, methodically loading tonight's meal of glorified TV dinners into several racks of warming ovens. The temperature in the plane drops almost instantly to the near freezing mark and within seconds; you could see your own breath. Needless to say, Mickey Mouse Airlines Inc. doesn't have a single blanket on board.

This is what you get for enlisting the services of the only airline left in the universe that still allows the smoking of coffin nails on a flight.

At 10:45, a full 3½ hours after our scheduled departure time, the captain delivers a garbled apology in a thick Arab accent, but can't be bothered to give any explanations. The ancient aircraft shudders in protest as our fearless leader applies full throttle to the power source, an overworked Rolls Royce that has surely been in action since the Eisenhower administration.

Something doesn't feel right ... not right at all.

I've flown enough to know when an aircraft ought to be achieving lift-off, and this flimsy, vomit-soaked beast clearly should be in the air by now. I glance at one of the flight attendants and could tell by the look on her perfect little Snow White face that I wasn't the only one who thought we were about to die. We barely clear the fence at the end of the runway and come within ten feet of clipping a row of dead oak trees due east of the airport.

Babies scream, the leper bows his head in silent prayer, the pilot mumbles, the mother jabs at her puke-stained, terry cloth pants suit, and 63 rows of nicotine junkies from all over the world simultaneously fire up their poison of choice.

11

NEVER MIND THE BOLLOCKS; IT'S 1986

Let's back up a decade. 1976. Do you remember how it was? If ya don't, consider yourself lucky. I had the right idea. I was on drugs.1976 was a banner year for polyester and leisure suits, and worse yet, all of America was defaced with red, white and blue. Mailboxes, cars, bicycles, even trees and houses. Is it any wonder that quaaludes were the drug of choice?

1976 was not a good year to be fucking around with cerebral drugs like LSD. Acid made you think. Quaaludes made you bounce down a flight of stairs like a deflated football and fuck your best friend's old lady while he was down at the gas station buying you more beer. 'Ludes made ya dumb, numb and oblivious. And they did one more thing — they made ya feel like Superman. In 1976, you needed all the delusions you could get.

For a moment, there appeared to be a ray of hope. After five years of sitting cross-legged on the floor in the time-honored "college position," motherfuckers wanted to dance again. I was all for it. "Fuck you all you Woodstock Zombies. Let's get up on that killing floor and do the boog-a-loo."

So, what do you think happens next? Yeah, they're dancing all right, but they're shaking their designer jeans asses to really lame shit like KC and the Sunshine Band and Loggins and Messina. Quick, gimme another 'lude. Thump, thump, thump, do the hustle, do the bump. Even the black groups were going all Wonder bread on me. I couldn't dance to this shit! Where was James Brown when I needed him? Wilson Pickett, can ya hear me? Clarence Carter, are ya out there somewhere "strokin?" C'mon Sly, get your nose outta that blow and show this flock of sheep what a dance groove feels like.

OK then, fuck the discos. Let's give the ole' radio dial a twist. Let's see what's happening on the airwaves. Uh oh, this is bleak. Same old overstuffed, out-of-touch bands, same old recycled Zep riffs. Sure man, pummel me with MORE Styx, REO, Head East, Bob Seger, Kansas, Journey … yer killin' me here. The Beagles ... err … I mean The Eagles. "Another Tequila Sunrise." Are you kidding me? My parents would like this shit. The Eagles' final sunrise couldn't come too soon for me. What a bunch of worthless hippie assholes. Maybe Manson will snap out of his madness long enough to execute all five of them. I wondered if I could live in a world where the Eagles sold more records than the Beatles?

Hey, I know. What's shakin' down south? Lotsa rich musical tradition down there. Nope. No luck. Wrong again. Nothin' doing here but the redneck outlaw invasion. Marshall Tucker, Molly Hatchet, The Outlaws and Charlie Daniels. This ain't rock 'n roll, this shit has fiddles in it! Hoo haw yeow!

The handwriting was on the rock and roll wall. The rock music that we had once known and loved was dead in the water, like stiff on arrival. Rock needed a new messiah, and there wasn't gonna be any help coming from Iggy's corner. Not yet, anyway. Iggy spent 1976 in a nuthouse, trying to save himself from his worst mortal enemy … himself.

Hey, I know, maybe Presley has another comeback left in him. Elvis? You gotta be joking. '76 Elvis was bloated like a toad and hadn't come out of his drug-addled coma in 15 long years. Elvis just tried to get through a day without shitting his jumpsuit.

There was some good stuff around if you knew where to look. Bowie, Slade, Aerosmith, Golden Earring, Roxy Music, T Rex, Modern Lovers and Lou Reed, but this was a mere ripple in a sea of vapid nothingness. I guess I wasn't that smart, though. I missed Big Star and The Flamin' Groovies, two bands that transcend the test of time.

The point I'm trying to make is this: Rock and roll, and all of pop culture for that matter, was at an all-time low in 1976, like down for the ten-count. And that was essential. It HAD to hit the absolute skids before people got pissed enough to push back. The so-called "punk explosion" couldn't have happened in 1973. The Stooges, New York Dolls and Dictators were living proof of that. Things weren't quite bad enough yet. The underground was starting to simmer and bubble, but it wasn't quite time to explode. By '76, people had had Barely Man-enuff, Donny and Marie, and Christopher Cross shoved down their throats once too often. People finally revolted against the apathy.

Suddenly, or so it seemed, there was a transformation on both sides of the mighty Atlantic. A new order, a voice of pissed-off juvenile delinquents, a revolution. Ramones, Damned, Stranglers, Sex Pistols, Clash, Generation X, Patti Smith Group, Television, Black Flag, Circle Jerks, Germs, Blondie, Heart-breakers. The floodgates were open, and the best part was, this shit was happening on a street level. Ten bands for ten bucks, CBGB's, leather pants, knee-high boots and haircuts that horrified parents. It was the '60s all over again.

Everybody started a band — loud, brash, bash it, trash it, out of tune, out of time, jack-hammer drums, hut 2-3-4. Some bands couldn't play so well. It didn't matter, It was okay, it was INSPIRED. Local scenes sprung up in all sectors of the world. Rock and roll mattered again. Iggy checked himself out of the rubber room and moved to Berlin to rub weenies with Bowie and released the minor masterpiece, "The Idiot." Punk began as a tiny snowball and steam-rolled its way up and over the button-down world and became an unstoppable avalanche. Sure, it failed commercially, but so what? That just lent further credence to the scene. This music was far too smart for the masses. Fuck 'em.

Now, ten years later, you can see Husker Dü on the Billboard charts and The Replacements on national TV. All is right with the world again, and we owe it all to Barely Man-enuff.

12

ROCKIN' AND RACIN'

So, listen here, there are only two things I ever wanted to do. I skipped the trip about being a cop or a fireman. I've always hated cops. Except for a brief period when I wanted to be a hired assassin, my vision has never wavered. Two things, just two lousy things. Yeah, okay, I'll tell ya. Indulge me for a second.

Oh, how I loved to make grownups squirm when they would ask me that universally dreaded question, "What do you wanna be when you grow up, little fella?"

"I wanna drive race cars and be a rock and roll star," I would insist with a sneer. It was perfect, and that's usually all it took to get 'em to stop stroking my little blonde head. Even then, I didn't trust adults.

Anyway, now I've grown up — haw haw — I'm a struggling (floundering?) pop star, and I still haven't driven an Indy Car. I've hot-lapped some sprint cars and raced a micro-sprint at a racetrack known as Angell Park, but that's it. If I don't accumulate my rock and roll fortune pretty damn soon, it's gonna be too late. I'm sick of waiting, and patience ain't no virtue in my book, not when you've dedicated your life to winning the Indianapolis 500 more times than that goddamn Foyt.

I did race go-karts in my teens, and I learned three things:

1) I'll do absolutely anything to win. Bang your best friend into the wall? No problem; cheating in racing is only cheating if ya get caught.

2) When it comes to going fast, I'm completely fearless. Somehow, I was born with the need for speed. My go-kart did 60 mph down the chutes on a dirt oval, but little Robbie wanted to go 120. Fast was never fast enough.

3) I'm a complete mechanical idiot. As good as I was as a driver, that's how bad I sucked with a wrench in my hand. I couldn't work on engines, I couldn't weld. I was hopeless, completely worthless. I just drove 'em until I crashed 'em, and then it was, "Daddy, I crashed again. I'm gonna need some more money."

Hence, I can forget mounting a competitive attack through the conventional route, which goes something like this: You build your first racecar with your bare fucking hands. Then you take insane chances on the track (no problem there) cuz your first racecar is always a bucket of greased shit. If you're any good, you get noticed by a well-to-do car owner who wants to win as bad as you do. Sadly, this ain't gonna work for me cuz, like I said, mechanically I'm a moron. No, building and repairing things just ain't my bag. I'm gonna have to buy everything: a completely assembled racecar, a tractor trailer, lotsa spare parts — hard chargers like me tend to crash a lot — and hell, probably the whole damn crew.

The problem is, that big-time rock and roll paycheck must be lost in the mail.

Having spent my entire life around racetracks and rock clubs, I've been able to draw some interesting parallels between these two sub-factions of our sicko society. Rockers and racers both have egos as vast as Siberia. Neither knows when it's time to quit. At least race drivers get killed or have their arms torn off in spectacular crashes. Rockers just hang around the scummy clubs they used to play in the '70s hoping to be remembered, sponging coke and cocktails and moaning about how they were "fucked over by their motherfucking manager or record company." "Man, I was on my way to mega-stardom but, _____." Fill in your own excuses; I'm sure you've been force fed every excuse in the universe.

Racers blame everybody but themselves when they aren't fast enough: the car owner, the crew, the race car, the tires, the motor, the chassis, the shocks, the torsion bars, other drivers and even the racetrack. Rockers blame the fans and tend to refer to their audiences as clueless farm animals or human baffle boards, constantly questioning their abilities for recognizing genius. I must say though, audiences can be hopeless idiots. Whoops, I did it, too. See how easy it is? I'm a pop genius and almost nobody noticed.

The parallels continue. Both usually lead stormy personal lives. A string of ex-wives, slutty groupies, hangers-on and bastard children are the rule rather than the exception. Kinda like the NBA. And then of course, there's the road. Greasy spoon diners, all-night drives, hangovers, too much coffee, pills to stay awake on and pills to go to sleep on and of course, zillions of cigarettes. Aw fuck yeah, such a healthy and happy lifestyle.

Rockers, like racers, only live to do what they do. Everything in between is just filler. Neither cope well with boredom. Rockers certainly don't have a patent on driving a Bentley into swimming pools, that's for sure. Sorry Keith Moon, may you rest in peace, but you're far from the only one. If anything, racers are even bigger brats than rock stars.

Finally, perhaps mercifully, both end up deaf as stones. Maybe that's so you can't hear all the nasty motherfucking that is sure to come your way when you've hung around too for long.

So there you have it. Look me up in 15-20 years. If all goes well, I'll be drowning in alimony payments. I'll be hustling drinks and neck deep in cocaine, still bitching like a banshee. I'll be working at a gas station or a 7-Eleven, maybe poopin' my rubber diaper in a nursing home, still looking for that one last ride.

Anybody need a deaf drummer or a racer who's had his arms torn off? I'll be around.

13

GETTING THERE

For what seemed like forever, I was obsessed with becoming a pop star.

I've had myself a decent little run out on the fringes of the rock frontier, and some might even say I even pulled it off. I swear I didn't buy drinks or drugs for like 20 years; other people bought them for me.

I've played on 23 records, gigged in 29 states and 14 countries and best of all, I got the girls. The extra smokin' hot with way too much blue eye shadow kind of girls, the ones who are drawn to the drummer cuz we're all so fucking reckless and broken and in need of fixing.

Nobody ever fixed me, but Christ did I let 'em try. I had the bad boy tragic poet act down pat. I'm almost ashamed to tell you how much action I got.

But in the end, rock stardom is a pile of steaming, stinking shit disguised as a diamond. It's a dog's life, and I'm glad I failed. It's little more than a handy excuse to live with your parents until you're thirty-fucking-five. It's all smoke and cocaine-laced mirrors, and in the end, what does it getcha?

It gets ya shot, overdosed, mutilated, mutated, humiliated, stoned, drunk, addicted, tripped out, schizophrenic, pornographic, forgotten, chewed-up, spit-out, spun out, scrutinized, glossed over, dropped, deemed irrelevant, divorced, deluded, degraded, secluded, jealous, wasted, spoiled, used up, washed out, deaf, dumb, and blinded by the lights.

It gets ya old before your time, crazed, lonely, lost, dazed, idolized, bitter, perverse, wired, tired, mired in mediocrity, bald, fat, out of time, out of shape, out of place, out of step, beaten, battered, barren, brutalized, bashed, bastardized, canonized, sterilized, plagiarized, jaded, maimed, egomaniacal, crippled, crashed, mashed, bashed, mangled, replaced, replacement hip surgery, cancer, toxic, venomous, dangerous repellent repulsive obtrusive obtuse obvious oblivious diphtheria polio mad-cow disease sickle cell anemia, cystic fibrosis, phobias for all occasions and "WE DON'T HEAR A SINGLE MOTHERFUCK-ER."

That's rock and roll, buddy boy, and ya better keep it comin' cuz I want me some more of that shit.

14

FOR RAY CHARLES (1930-2004)

Here's a travesty for ya: Brother Ray is dead at 73, and the "liberal media" spends a whole week frothing at the mouth with an endless barrage of Ronnie Raygun flim-flam, while reducing the great Ray Charles to a mere footnote.

This is what happens when you have the misfortune of dying on the same day as a somehow beloved ex-president.

For those of us with our hearts and souls still in the right place, we know the score. Charles was the high priest of American soul music, and he was more important, more relevant and goddamn it, a BETTER AMERICAN than that B-movie hack who sweet-talked an asleep-at-the-wheel nation into giving him the job as Commander in Chief some 30-odd years ago.

Ray Charles' skills as a songwriter, piano player, band leader, producer, singer and arranger were practically unparalleled, and his complete mastery of every genre he tackled is unrivaled in the history of pop music. His voice spoke to millions, and there is no higher degree of respect than the outpouring of love shown him by his contemporaries.

"When Ray started singing, that was it. Everybody else was picking up the scraps," said no less than fellow legend Little Stevie Wonder. One of his many nicknames perhaps said it best.

His friends referred to him simply as "the genius."

Brother Ray
    i wanna go where you go
    i wanna know what you know
    brother ray
    i wanna feel what you feel
    brother ray can we make a deal?
    i'll sell my soul for ya
    brother ray
    i wanna see what you see
    i feel your mojo when i sleep
    you're such a shoo shoo baby
    brother ray
    you got them x-ray blues
    ain't no colors in the truth
    you're king daddy magic
    brother ray

15

TALES FROM THE CRYPT OF A
WORKING CLASS HERO (1993)

Fri. 9-21

Uh oh, now I've done it, working in a factory for a lousy $5.50 an hour —
the new kid on the block, the low man on an already toppling totem pole. Are
the workers as miserable as I think they should be? It doesn't seem so. Maybe
they like it here. It's probably too early to make such sweeping generalizations,
but nobody here seems very bright. I concede that this is what I get for resort-
ing to a temp agency for work. Except for my brief tenure as a concrete worker
(from which I bear permanent scars from third-degree chemical burns), and the
sheer hell that is hanging drywall, this looks to be by far the most physically demanding gig I've ever had, and certainly the least stimulating, mentally. Lucky
for me, I'm perversely attracted to physically taxing jobs, it keeps my drummer
muscles in rippled like a blacksmith's.

Sat. 9-22

Volunteered for a five-hour stint. Got up at 4:45, bought a paper (if you can
call the Saturday edition of the Milwaukee Sentinel a paper), and slammed a
pot of black coffee. There are no surprises in this work. Having just gotten fired
from an ultra-stressful job with Wisconsin Electric where one false location of
underground cable could flip a bulldozer and get somebody killed, the absence
of life-and-death anxiety is a welcome reprieve.

Sun. 9-23

No work. Watched pro football. Drank beer. Just another cog in the wheel.
Just one more worthless piece of blue-collar white trash.

Mon. 9-24

Blue mother Monday. This, I find out the hard way, is not the kind of job
that you wanna work while hungover. Too noisy, dirty and hard. It's likely that
this awful place will create a strong get-drunk impulse. Soon, I'll probably be
sitting in some corner juke joint after work, muttering angrily into my scotch
and water. God help me. It's a 16-mile commute one way, 12 of which is ex-
pressway. Today I really gassed my '81 Volvo station wagon, still wounded
from an earlier hit-and-run accident where I t-boned a limousine with a coked-
to-the-gills Billy Joel inside, and made it to work in 19 minutes flat. I call my
ride "the Swedish Meatball," and the front end is so cockeyed from the crash,
it feels like it's constantly trying to veer into oncoming traffic and kill me.

And it probably is. This goddamn car has been going all "Christine" on me from the moment I first laid eyes on it. I now know that I can stay in bed until 6:30 and still make it to work on time. Get up, use the toilet, brush teeth, don solvent-soaked factory clothes and try to run 80 mph without getting myself busted or killed. Nobody bothers to try and look good here.

Tues. 9-25
Sameness. Drudgery. Check your mind at the door. Become an anonymous worker bee, a drone. Only two people know my name; I revel in that.

Wed. 9-26
Everybody here is a man, except for two. There's a butchy woman of about 60 with hands like a bricklayer and not a trace of estrogen left in her DNA. She has been here for like 35 years. The other female, a Chinese American in her early 20s, is a real dish and attracts a lot of attention. I aspire to bang her, but she seems to hate me. "Prove yourself boy," the sidelong glances seem to be saying. Show us you're cut from the same cloth as us, which of course I'm not. I really don't mind this form of rejection. This place completely shuts down during opening day of deer season, so there ya go.

Thurs. 9-27
I'm jotting down daily entries, written on the sly in a spiral notebook I keep hidden under a trash barrel. This is grounds for dismissal, but I don't care.

I guess I should explain what it is I do around here, in all its mundane glory. First, I run parts through a revolving cylinder, officially known as the "hopper," which resembles an Apollo space capsule. I wish it were so I could fly the fuck away. The hopper contains 40 gallons of scalding water cut with generic industrial soap. I backwash the parts for three to five minutes before throwing the reverse mechanism and dropping my little metal slugs into a wire-mesh basket where they await a dip into what appears to be a kerosene based solution. What effect does this liquid death have on my liver and lungs if it can eat through a pair of rubber gloves in two days? I try not to contemplate this.

Out comes the 45-pound basket. A couple of vigorous shakes separates the solvent from the parts. I call this process "shaking the juice loose," but it also succeeds in shaking the tendons loose from my forearms. We can now add pain to my growing list of grievances. Next, I pitch the product onto a drying tray. Repeat process endlessly. Rinse, lather, repeat and see if you snap.

While this is happening, I funnel the parts into a bag-lined box. Weigh, seal, shut, mark for shipment and stack boxes eight high on a 3-by-4-foot skid. It's amazing how stupid you can get after doing this for eight hours. I smoke the daily quota, something the Suits don't expect from a novice who has been on the job for a mere six days. It's my only motivation.

Fri. 9-28
A week lasts a month around here. A tuna fish and potato chips lunch highlights my day. How sad is that? Only three of us don't smoke around here: the

Chinese girl, myself and a future sniper of America named Duane. More on that whack-a-doodle later. And oh, several machinists are missing fingers.

Mon. 10-1

A whirlwind of rock and roll and fatigue; a fueled-by-booze and kind bud kind of weekend. I seem to require the release of playing live shows now more than ever before. By Sunday night, I'm beginning to feel good again, but then the dull ache of despair that used to haunt me as a schoolboy hits me right between my eyes. Face it boy, fun time is over.

Tues. 10-2

This place is all about urgency. Machinery in motion. Busy, busy, busy. Pulsing and breathing, creating the illusion that our economy is working. Neither my supervisor, Fred, nor anybody else I ask have a clue what Hilti half-inch expander plugs are for, but they must be important considering how feverishly we are cranking them out. It's just another tiny piece of the grand scheme. Grand scam is more like it.

Wed. 10-3

Today, I decided to dance to the polyrhythmic beat of the machinery. I'd estimate it's about 90 beats per minute, a deep groove, kinda like Afrika Bambaataa. When my mood is good, which is rare, it soothes. I try not to resent the factory agenda, which is all about the bottom line, production at all costs. That's not easy for me. I just shut up and get the job done. If I wanna flex my big-ass personality, I can go get a fucking sales job.

Thurs. 10-4

A couple of guys are starting to act familiar with me. Familiar, but not friendly. I'd prefer to remain anonymous. The MAN around here is named Joe. I haven't seen him yet, but he's considered a prick and a tyrant. His intimidating voice, a thundering drone, booms over the crude sound system dozens of times each day, the voice of GOD. "Dewey, see Joe." So far, T.J., a forklift driver, is my lone ally. Youngish and just smart enough to realize that if you stay here long enough, you'll never get out, T.J. dreams of a job in radio. Yeah, "T.J. the DJ" has a nice ring to it. He warns me not to get on Joe's bad side.

Fri. 10-5

The workers around here have a greenish gray pallor to their skin. It may be Friday, but I feel no semblance of a Friday buzz. Fred begs me to pull a five-hour shift on Saturday. I tell him I'd sooner set myself on fire.

Mon.10-8

I feel purged since my glammed-out power-pop band, Love Bully, played Rockford on Friday and Madison on Saturday. We were hitting on all cylinders, but it's getting harder than ever to face this god-awful place. I got a compliment today from a co-worker named Mikey. "Hey you little cocksucker, you cost me

20 bucks. I bet Fred you wouldn't show up anymore after last Friday. You're a tougher motherfucker than we all thought." "Gee, thanks, Mikey," I said sarcastically, but it sailed right over his head.

Tues. 10-9

Got busted twice today by my supervisor, Fred. It's hard enough to take him seriously to begin with, but his severe speech impediment makes it all the harder. The first bust was for daring to sit down while I sorted parts. The alternative is to bend over from the waist for eight straight hours until your back is trashed. Bust number two was for incorrectly boxing J-hooks. The second Fred walked away, I committed my first act of open defiance and resumed with my subversive method. Somewhere, a stooge with a clipboard probably wrote down my transgression.

Wed. 10-10

I gave myself a good, stern lashing about not seeking a new job. Truth is, I'm too tired and depressed to bother. What's with me? I have a college degree. I have options. Perhaps this is what I get for putting all of my eggs in the rock and roll basket. Jesus Christ, maybe my parents were right when they told me I needed to have something to fall back on in case things didn't pan out in music. Still and all, on a purely creative level, I am by and large satisfied. I write songs, I sing, I play drums, and I lead my very own semi-successful regional band. I've written some good songs, made some decent records, done some touring, even enjoyed some critical acclaim and maybe even what you might term lower-echelon commercial success.

I've worked hard and stayed focused honing my craft; a noble gesture, right? Yeah, okay, rock and roll is a tough racket if you care about money (and I do), one of the toughest of all rackets when ya think about it. I feel good knowing that here I am, still down in the rock and roll trenches slugging away. I've taken my lumps without complaint, the near misses, the setbacks, the hassles, the lousy shows, the starting over from scratch.

Bring it on. I'm a warrior. I can take it. But this? I dunno, man. My working life is a rapidly worsening downward spiral. It's getting harder each year to juggle a job and a "career" that sometimes feels more like an expensive hobby, or on my worst days, a crash course in sheer futility. I've had a few jobs that had what I guess you could call "career potential," and that was even worse. Thanks, but no thanks. Going back to the rat race that is media sales is not an option, which brings us right back to square fucking one. What the hell else, besides being in a band do I wanna do?

The answer, of course, is NOTHING. But what a price to pay. I've never, ever made a living at this unless you wanna count the six months I spent on the road with Janus Green and Jones. I was Jones cuz these fucking idiots burned through so many drummers they got sick of changing their name every three weeks. We were a "variety band," which is slick talk code for monkey suit wearing human jukebox lounge lizards, grinding out the hits four sets a night, six nights a week in every faceless Formica and leatherette joint from Iron

Mountain, Michigan, to Pine Bluff, Arkansas. One time, we had to drive 800 miles on our only day off, and I was trapped in an International Harvester Wagoneer with these two bitter, road weary crispy critters. To make matters even worse, it was the dead of summer, and somehow the heater was stuck on wide open. It's the closest to suicide I've ever gotten, and I quit after three months in Bob Dylan's hometown (Hibbing, Minnesota) with my dignity barely intact.

Since then, I've driven trucks, installed aluminum siding, tended bar, waited tables, wrote and sold TV spots, delivered food specialty items to grocery stores, worked as a shipping/receiving clerk at a hospital, freelanced for some racing periodicals and several other jobs too inconsequential or short-term to even mention. Am I versatile or just plain lost? And now … this! Three lousy weeks and I'm cracking, nerves frayed, losing it. I'm too sensitive for this place. All I see are broken spirits, oppression and drudgery. All they do is work, drink and kill animals. I'm certain that some of these guys beat their wives. It frightens me to look too long into the eyes of these men. All I sense is barely bottled rage and weary resignation. Nobody around here gets treated with any respect, and I know that sooner or later some of these rednecks are gonna blow their fucking corks on somebody. Most likely me.

Thur. 10-11
Fred, who happens to be a black man, was impressed when he heard me playing "James Brown, Live at the Apollo" on my pimped out boom-box, and wanted to know what a little white-boy like me was doing listening to the Godfather. Ignoring the racial jab, I let him know that I admired all kinds of black music and ticked off some of my favorites: Al Green, Sly Stone, Smokey Robinson, Wilson Pickett, Marvin Gaye, The Spinners, Temptations, Four Tops, Clarence Carter and several others. Fred just shook his head and said, "You don't play that punk rock shit do you?" This is where the conversation ground to a halt.

Fri. 10-12
A machinist who runs a press down by the candy machine thinks I'm happy just cuz I sing at work, so he's taken to calling me Frank, as in Sinatra. We now have a standard dialogue. Dickie says, "Rub my sweaty tits, Frank." In response I sing, "Shoobie Doobie Do," from "Strangers in the Night."

Mon. 10-16
Sick. To death.

Tues. 10-17
Sick again. Feel like shit, but still better than being well at work.

Wed. 10-18
Called in again. Looked at the classifieds, but too depressed to act on anything.

Thurs. 10-19

The world is now three days behind its demand for Hilti half-inch expander plugs. How will the economy ever possibly recover? It feels good to break the rules and write a letter to the mother of my 2-year-old son when no one — that I know of — is looking. It's a "dear john" letter and it's a day that just wouldn't end.

Fri. 10-20

I think I mentioned Duane earlier. Lonely, angry dullard, almost 30, has worked here since he graduated from high school. Hates his life and himself. Stutters when agitated, which is often. I try to be kind to him, though I sense some serious psycho potential. His girlfriend of seven years has just thrown him overboard for a nursing home cafeteria worker. He's confided in me about this. While Duane busies himself with a UPS order, I start tossing expander plugs in his general direction about 40 feet away, just to kill the Friday boredom. I keep this going for half an hour, stepping up my attack before Duane gets wise. INSTANT BERSERKO. Duane throws down his tape gun and makes a bee-line straight for me. He's a big guy with meat slabs for hands, but I'm more than ready and willing to rock with this hostile fuck. Bring it, man! Fred and Mike pull us apart, and Duane gets a three-day suspension and threatens my life on the way out. I'm not so lucky. I get a verbal warning. Some days you can't do anything right.

Mon. 10-23

Damn. Against all odds, I write one of the best songs of my life today. My bass player, Steve, who also works in a factory, swears that he writes his best stuff at work, but I never believed it could be true. I wanted to show "Empty Handed Again" to somebody, but quickly realized that no one would care. God knows why, but this bothered me so much that I hid in the can for 20 minutes bawling like a newborn. It felt terrific.

Tues. 10-24

Had a good, sweaty, slippin' and slidin' rock and roll show last night at Hooligan's Super Bar. Now I know why I keep jumping through barbed-wire hoops to do this. I call in with a lame excuse about car trouble and sleep until 9:30.

Wed. 10-25

There's a guy in my department who's a really sick fucker. He calls me his little blonde bitch, and I don't think he's kidding. I'm sure he's gay. But if he ever admitted it to himself, I'm sure he would slash his wrists. I call him "sweetie." This shows you how starved I am for stimulus.

Thurs. 10-26

Like every factory everywhere, I'm sure, we have our token heavy metal rock star. And just my fucking luck, he's a drummer, and he somehow found out that I'm one, too. He struts by my section every damn day all heavy-lidded stare and blue eye shadow with his fringy leatherette jacket and puffy West Allis hair that makes him look like a blonde French poodle. He tells me he has a $3,600 Pearl cage kit with 16 pieces, so I already know that we've got nothing in common. I'll bet my beloved '59 Ludwigs that his favorite drummer is Neal Peart. I figure I'll tell him that my favorite drummers are Ringo and Charlie Watts and that anything over four pieces confuses me, and he'll never talk to me again.

Fri. 10-27

Awoke to a high-compression agitation, which only worsens as I await my ten-minute morning candy bar and coffee break. A horrible rash has developed on my thighs from wearing my kerosene-soaked jeans too many times between washings. My back is killing me, and the machinery clatter-trap sounds like it's mocking me — metal grinding on metal.

And me? It's bone grinding on bone with no toolbox in the world to fix what ails me. Joe drones. The heavy metal peacock struts. Dickie talks trash. T.J. dreams. Duane smolders. Fred stutters. And I silently slip out the side door and never look back.

16

WHEN SEX IS REMOVED FROM FOOTBALL

I'm still a sucker for high school football. I've never gotten over it and likely never will. Even progress can't kill this proud and noble grand American tradition. In certain sectors of the country, but particularly in Iowa, Ohio, Texas and Pennsylvania, high school football lives in the hearts of its citizens right alongside God, the bomb and Walmart.

High school football isn't a sport, it's a religion.

I was on a routine cigarette score when I spied the time-honored Friday night lights. Hot damn — I was in business, a football game. My heart raced, then sank like a stone. Suspicion set in. This wasn't the same America that I had once known and loved, not by a longshot. It probably wasn't football after all; it was just as likely a goddamn soccer game. Call me provincial, but I hate soccer with every fiber of what's left of me.

But this time, the gods were with me. The gods who play rock and roll with Fender and Gibson guitars and four-piece Ludwig drum kits The gods who know that racing means single-seat, open-cockpit race cars that only turn left, race on dirt and mount their engines in the front. The gods who put giant fins on Cadillacs. The gods who let high school kids play football under the lights on Friday nights.

Nickel defenses, triple options, blitzing linebackers (like I once was), goal-line stands and adrenaline-charged kids dressed as medieval warriors trying to cripple each for life. Hell yes, this is the America that I call home!

So who the hell's playing? Who fucking cares? The scoreboard told me all I needed to know: VISITORS 7 HOME 0. It was still the first quarter. I sprinted for the ticket window and plunked down my three bucks. Awesome! Affordable family fun in the form of barely controlled violence. I was alive, ripe for the vibe. I was 17. I was a Mt. Pleasant Panther again, and I wanted to knock somebody clean out of their shoes.

Right away, there was trouble. I bought a cup of crummy coffee, fired up a Marlboro light and settled in. Instantly, a full three rows of mortified suburbanites spun around as if on cue and beheld me with a mixture of contempt and disbelief. As I scanned my brainwaves for an explanation, SHE arose from the bleachers like a toxic weed, hands placed defiantly on her cheese-fed hips, her laser beam eyes oozing pure purple poison.

She condescendingly addressed me with a voice that cut like an off-key soprano: "YOUNG MAN, EXTINGUISH THAT CIGARETTE THIS INSTANT OR I SHALL BE FORCED TO SUMMON THE POLICE AND HAVE YOU ARRESTED. DON'T YOU REALIZE THAT SMOKING ON SCHOOL

GROUNDS IS A CRIME?"

"What? No ... I was just … you're trying to tell me that smoking cigs is a crime? Jesus Christ. lady, we're outside," I whined.

Great Gawd almighty. I had been rendered defenseless by what appeared to be the poster bitch for menopause, and what was I gonna do about it? As I groped in vain for a face-saving comeback, she plopped her fat ass down as a chorus of "way to go, Sarah" and "that's telling him" hung in the autumn air like mustard gas. Only my devout love for the game kept me from bolting for my car to smoke some kind bud to scrub this nightmare away in a cloud of smoke.

My devotion to football could never be questioned. When I was in high school, I had WILLED myself a football player, a 5-foot-9, 135-pound line-backer — the runt of the litter who survived only by being as mean and nasty of a sackful of rattlesnakes. I'd even had the team doctor tell me I had to quit, that I was one wrong hit away from paralysis. I told him to fuck off and only missed one game. I played dirty, but I played tough, and I just lived to hit and hurt people. By senior year, I had earned myself a reputation as a genuine bad-assed headhunter and had earned a nickname that any footballer would be proud of: "THE ASSASSIN." I'd had cracked ribs, a hairline vertebra fracture, torn ligaments and pinched nerves, so I wasn't about to let some upper-crust, middle-aged hag bully me out of the stands with a verbal stiff arm.

So fuck her.

I turned my attention back to the game, but this was the sorriest excuse for high school football I had ever seen. There was no atmosphere, no intensity, no hatred and no magic. Football isn't supposed to be a polite game. Good manners ain't required. Where was the violence? Didn't these boys have any goddamn testosterone?

Just before the half, Shorewood scored on a 17-yard screen pass to tie the score at 7. This in itself was a miracle. Shorewood had twice had the longest losing streak in Wisconsin high school football history. Their program was in such shambles that when they hired a new coach in 2007, he declared the team so anemic, he demanded that they take a year off to regroup. As a result, my son, Sean, who was a senior at the time, was force fed a soccer game for home-coming. Sean skipped the game. That's my boy! After the touchdown, the band played their crummy school fight song, and the crowd cheered half-heartedly.

And that's when it hit me. I was jolted loose from my mind by a cruel dose of postmodern reality. No wonder this game was more like a tiptoe through the fucking tulips than a bone-jarring exercise in teen fury. Sex had been removed from the equation. Neither team had cheerleaders. And that's when I'd seen quite enough. Another grand American tradition ground into the dirt under the politically correct boot heel. The goddamn squares had won another round.

I stopped at the ticket window on the way out. I just had to know.

"Yeah, excuse me," I said to the woman who looked like an oversized chickenhawk, "how come there ain't any cheerleaders?"

"Cheerleaders?" said the long-beaked ticket taker. She sounded more than a trifle testy.

"Yeah, you know, pompons and rah-rahs. Where the hell are they?""Young man, we abolished cheerleaders five years ago."

She was trying to sound polite, but you could tell it was a stretch.

"Cheerleading is sexist," she continued. "We were the first school in the Little Ten to abolish them. Now, none of the schools in our conference have them anymore."

She sounded real pleased with herself, like she'd discovered a cure for cancer or something. I stumbled away, numb, dumb, bewildered and resigned to eternal misery.

When I made it to the relative safety of my car, I reached for the glove box and pulled out a half-gone pint of Maker's Mark whiskey. I raised the poisonous potion to my lips and drank a silent, angry toast to the death of yet another sacred cow.

17

MEIN BLOWN

So, there I was dressed up as Hitler snorting cocaine off the bar. No really, I couldn't make this stuff up. I was a textbook case of what sociologists would refer to as "a breaching experiment," decked out in full Nazi regalia complete with knee-high patent-leather jack-boots and armband swastika.

The night was still young, and already, allies were getting hard to come by, except for a gay rock and roll singer with third-tier talent who had followed me into the can.

"I'm a sucker for a man in a uniform," lisped the poser with the fucking nerve to call himself "Billy Bomb." About the only thing "bomb" about Billy was his act. He had nuthin.'

The fact that it was Halloween night didn't seem to be buying me much slack with the public at large, either. Within moments of leaving my house, I'd been threatened by an Arab cashier at the Open Pantry who refused to sell me a pack of Chesterfield Kings.

But fuck that and fuck him, too!

I had two C-notes sunk into the uniform alone, I was slipping deeper into character with each cocktail and now, the bartender was inexplicably feeding me lines of pure pharmaceutical cocaine right there at the bar. I didn't mind. I hit it like a high-end Hoover.

So what's a deranged fuhrer to do, but ignore the faint whispers of reason in his drug-fueled brain?

The dirty looks and hurled insults were starting to come fast and furious now, and any minute, I was gonna need another line just to keep pace with all the hostility. I could sense an overthrow brewing from the far end of the horse-shoe-shaped bar. I pondered my options and quickly decided that a quiet retreat wasn't one of 'em. "I'M ADOLPH FUCKING HITLER AND I DON'T BACK DOWN FOR NOBODY," I shouted "SIEG HEIL!"

Another line of blow appeared, and my fate was sealed and delivered. I figured there was no reason to fuck around half-heartedly. If I was gonna be Hitler, goddamn it, I was gonna BE Hitler. Fueled by powdered courage, reckless arrogance and several extra-dry gin martinis, I spun off my bar stool and goose-stepped straight to the red and purple jukebox. "Dead Babies," by Alice Cooper, a very Hitleresque selection, I thought.

Timely exits and sound judgement have never been my strong suits, and when yet another small mountain of Peruvian marching powder appeared before me, I was beyond all reason.

"I gotta admit it, fella," muttered the bartender, "you got some fuckin' balls of brass."

This coming from a bartender who routinely fed his barflies pure cocaine for happy hour. Feeling vindicated, I climbed atop the bar, toasted the room, and began to deliver an impassioned yet rambling speech about the rise of the Third Reich and my warped vision for global domination. In the full clutches of my dope frenzy, I thought I was being ironic and satirical. The Three Stooges had gotten away with lampooning Hitler, and so had Mel Brooks. So why couldn't I? I wasn't gonna exterminate any Jews or anything; I just wanted to have some fun.

I quickly realized that the booze and the drugs had skewered my normally crack comedic timing and moreover, even an Academy Award-winning performance couldn't possibly overshadow the stigma of my being Adolph Hitler.

It was a joke nobody got but me.

By the time I realized that people find Hitler about as funny as stomach cancer, it was too fuckin' late.

Suddenly, with all the deftness of an acrobat having a grand mal seizure, I was dodging an arsenal of ashtrays, beer mugs, Candy corn and death threats. In a desperate last-ditch attempt to get out on a high note, I leaped down off the bar and blindsided some dumb schmuck wearing a rubber Ronald Reagan mask with my switchblade pocket comb. Apparently, Ray-guns wanted no part in playing my personal political punching bag, and without so much as a flinch, he dumped his pitcher of Blatz on my head and followed through with a perfectly placed scissors-kick to my five-star dictator balls.

The crowd erupted in thunderous applause as I dropped to my knees, whimpering like a third-grade school girl. Clearly, the party was over and not a comrade in sight. Score another round for the divine Western world superpowers.

And that's when it hit me, a final lucid moment amidst the chaos. This must be close to what the real Hitler had felt like when the grim reality of his own cock-eyed delusions had hit him right between his fascist fucking eyes.

In the end, the life of a Nazi war-monger comes down to this: you're all dressed up, ya got nowhere to go.

18

UP AND DOWN THE $ MONEY $ GO ROUND

This is getting clear outta hand, I'm notorious — a legend — and for all the wrong reasons. These days, I get greeted with words like "Hi Rob, haven't seen you in a while. Been fired lately?" "Hey, Rob, what's new? Between jobs again?"

"Aw, shut the fuck up, I'm looking for new career opportunities. I got canned again."

Loud guffaws, snickers. "What's new about that? You always get fired."

My friends don't even pretend to be surprised anymore. Christ, at least they could humor me. But there were no "tough breaks" or "too bads" coming my way from their corner, or any corner for that matter. No, just the same old knowing glances and rolling eyes, the same old wise guy remarks.

One night, I announced to a few of my drinking buddies that I was gonna be starting a new job, and the crummy bastards started layin' down bets right there on the spot.

"I'll give ya five to one he don't last 90 days," cracked Craig with his famed arrogance. Hysterical laughter bounced off the tavern walls.

"You'd have to be nuts to take a bet like that," answered a smirking Mikey as he gulped for oxygen between laughing fits.

"I'll betcha he don't last 30 days," Craig challenged. "And I'll give ya four to one."

I winced as my so-called friends poured it on.

"Rob even got fired by the city, and they never fire anybody. My stupid cousin, Antonio, has an IQ of 43 and has a wooden leg, and even he can't get fired."

Now the whole bar was getting into the act.

"Yeah, my cousin was at Pizza Heaven the time Rob turned a table over on a customer cuz they complained that they didn't get enough sausage on their pizza."

Everyone cackled wickedly as I felt my blood pressure begin to accelerate.

"Yeah, and what about that time Rob was driving for Yellow Cab and he shoved a used diaper in that mother's face cuz she was a buck fifty short?"

"I'll give ya two to one he doesn't last 90 days." cracked Mikey. Hysterical laughter once again echoed through the bar.

"All right! Shut the hell up! That's enough. I'll take that bet," I screeched.

The barroom went instantly still. A room full of pop rivet eyes drilled me to the floor.

"What did you say?" asked Craig with barely suppressed laughter.

"You heard me. A grand says I last 90 days. Another thousand says I'm still around in 120."

Suddenly, the joint began to resemble the trading floor at the New York Stock Exchange. Everyone was shouting at once, wanting a piece of my action. The line slid up and down like a Vegas title bout. Motherfuckers I didn't even know were lining up to bet against me.

"Easy money; who wants in?" Mikey shouted, assuming the role of pit boss. When the dust had cleared, the odds settled at three to one that I couldn't stick. All I had to do was keep this one lousy waiter job for four months, and I'd be raking in enough scratch to make a deal on a used Sportster I'd had my eye on and still have enough left over for an extended trip to Greece. My cut would be a cool $6,700 and change versus the $2,200 I would have to cough up should the unthinkable happen. This should prove to be all the incentive I should need, I thought.

But later, as I lie awake doing a mental replay of my sordid job history, I caught myself wishing I had held out for bigger numbers. Much bigger numbers. Logic was telling me that the odds were closer to ten to one. I hadn't held a job for three months in 17 years, and my tolerance level was lower than ever. People! They're the worst. Me and my big fucking mouth.

Sometimes, it makes me nervous that my friends know me so well. I mean, it's bad enough that they know that me fucking up and getting the hatchet is inevitable, but what really pisses me off is that they can so accurately predict why.

"So Rob, heard ya got fired again. What'd ya do, smack another customer?"

"Certainly not," I said with as much dignity as I could muster. "I learn from my mistakes. This time it was a simple case of insubordination."

"Oh, you smacked your boss, huh?"

I hate it when my friends can peg me. It makes me feel so goddamn predictable. I'm thinking about moving to Oklahoma, where being a hothead is more socially acceptable.

I started my new job with a newfound determination. I played it straight, straighter than I ever thought possible. I did my job with quiet efficiency and maximum ass kissing. I avoided controversy at all costs and was careful to never say an unkind word to anyone. One night, I bitch slapped the chef over a scalloped potato incident, but that quickly blew over.

I "yes sir'ed" and "no maam'ed" my way straight through my first 90 days without so much as an incident. I tried in vain to ignore all the side-effects of all this lily-white, goody two-shoes behavior. The problem was, I was losing my self-respect. True enough, I wasn't alienating anybody, but I wasn't making anybody laugh, either. I was lulling myself into a catatonic state.

"Use it or lose it," as the saying went, and I hadn't snarled at anyone in three long months. I began to fear that I was losing my edge. Sarcasm was my best sport, and being pleasant was making me itchy. I did, however, begin to notice that my friends were starting to get twitchy, and that made me feel a whole lot better.

"I hear you're still working at Mr. Ed's," said Mikey nervously.

"That's right, buddy boy," I countered with certainty, "and I was employee of the month in May, too. I've already made my reservations for Greece, and I'm having my Harley shipped over," I added, twisting the knife in his back.

On Day 113, a Friday, six of my friends who just happened to have a vested interest in my job fate, made dinner reservations at Ed's, and made a big deal out of demanding to be seated in my section. I was ready for the evil bastards. They tried everything to unnerve me, from hurling forks to trying to trip me while I was carrying a tray full of drinks. I figured that if they wanted to play dirty pool, I could play that game, too. After Craig yelled, "Hey pretty boy, still sucking cocks at the bus station!?" I had them tossed out like old tennis shoes. Loyalty means nothing to me when there's almost seven grand at stake.

Day 117, a Monday, just three crummy days away from the largest payoff of my life, we had a phenomenal dinner rush. A cook and dishwasher had already quit on the spot, and our best waitress was found cowering in the meat locker. I had nine of my own tables and had cheerfully volunteered to pick up the rest of Gail's until, if, and when she agreed to come out of the locker. I didn't care. I was all but on my way to Greece.

By 10:30, things had settled to a dull roar. I was working my last four tables and was looking forward to a late night of cards, girls and whiskey on the rocks. I was especially enjoying a four-top of sweet old nuns from St. Francis Parish who were pushing the ritual of drinking Christ's bloods to new levels of commitment. The old girls were drinking like pirates and were well into their fifth carafe of port before they asked for their check. I was still in unusually high spirits and had even dared to allow a glimpse of my old self to come shining through. I fired off several snappy one liners, much to the sisters' delight I might add, and one had even complimented me on what a personable young lad I was. The ole bats were in the palm of my hand.

Maybe I got reckless, but even in retrospect, I'm much more inclined to think that the wine had made 'em mean. These ladies had clearly shown a sense of humor, so I'm still at a loss to explain how they could've turned on me so completely.

"I'm so full, I may have to walk back to the parish tonight to work off all these calories," Sister Arlene sighed with a smile.

I laughed aloud, "Aw, just rap a few extra kids across the back of the knuckles with your ruler tomorrow. That'll get ya back down to playing weight."

The smile was gone in a split instant. In its place was a menacing scowl. I knew immediately that this spelled trouble. I braced myself for the onslaught.

"Young man, I will have you know that in 33 years of teaching, I have never once struck a child. Now, I strongly suggest you bring us our change this instant, and while you're at it, I demand a word with your manager!"

"But ... but ... but, sister," I stammered. "I was only joking. Please, you've got to believe me, I didn't mean any harm. I'm terribly sorry if I offended you."

I was making myself sick from this syrupy, half-hearted apology, but damage control was my only hope.

"I'm afraid it's a little late for apologies, young man," she hissed through clenched teeth. "You've not only insulted me personally, but you've managed to insult the entire Catholic church and everything it stands for. NOW LET ME

TALK TO YOUR MANAGER. NOW!"

"Fucking drunken wino penguin," I muttered under my breath as I turned away.

"I HEARD THAT, YOU LITTLE SMART ALEC. I WILL NOT TOLERATE YOUR FILTHY MOUTH AND BAD ATTITUDE FOR ANOTHER INSTANT. YOU CAN'T TALK TO ME LIKE THAT. I'M A NUN!"

The whole dining room went as eerily silent as a graveyard. I stared at my shoes and said a silent, desperate prayer. My manager marched briskly to the trouble spot and stiffly introduced herself, "Hello, I'm Lucy, the night shift manager. Is there a problem with your service?"

"I'LL SAY THERE'S A PROBLEM," the nun bellowed. "THIS … THIS … THIS … BOY HAD THE AUDACITY TO CALL ME A FUCKING WINO PENGUIN!"

The entire room let out a collective gasp like you hear at the circus when the crowd thinks the high wire artist is gonna splatter all over the sawdust. Lucy shot me darts through slitted, cat green eyes.

"YOU'RE FIRED. STARTING NOW! YOU'RE THE LOWEST. I KNEW YOU WERE TROUBLE WHEN I HIRED YOU. HOW COULD YOU? NOW GET OUT!"

The dining room broke into thunderous applause as I grasped in vain for some face-saving words. I flung myself onto the floor and began to babble hysterically.

"My Harley. What about my Harley? Three days, just three fuckin' days. I almost had it. Seven grand up in smoke. YOU CAN'T DO THIS TO ME. WHERE AM I GONNA GET 2,200 BUCKS WITHOUT A FUCKING JOB? NOW I'LL NEVER GET A HARLEY. THERE'S NO GOD OR JESUS OR MOTHER MARY. I HOPE THE POPE DIES TONIGHT. YOU CAN'T DO THIS TO ME. THE PENGUIN'S A LIAR!" I wailed, kicking and twitching like a dying dog.

"Oh my God, he's having a seizure," I heard someone say through my delirium. "Quick, somebody do something!"

"He's insane," proclaimed someone else assuredly. Suddenly, three patrons leaped on me and frantically tied up my arms and legs with their neckties. I lie there like a roped rodeo calf, helpless.

I was still thrashing about on the floor, still raving about Greece and revenge and the Harley that would never be when the paramedics arrived and jabbed me with a syringe full of liquid bliss — pure morphine.

"I'll get you, Penguin," I managed through the drug haze before I smacked head-on into the welcome wall of sweet, deep sleep.

19

THE LAST RESORT INN

I'm partial to the kind of joints where people mutter into their drinks. Bitter, belligerent, seething, cut ya soon as look at ya down on their luck motherfuckers with skin the color of aged concrete. Bleak, but irrepressible. Life keeps on beating 'em up, but they never back down.

They still got their smell.

No matter how bitter their sorry ass lives get, no matter how fucked up shit gets, no matter how many times life kicks 'em to the curb, they keep on comin' back for more. Beef jerky, whiskey straight from the rail, Merle Haggard on the jukebox and a rack of nine-ball for ten bucks a pop.

You can't fake this shit, and it ain't for sale, either. Forget about the Marlboro Man. He was a fuckin' pussy. The kind of guys I'm talkin' about could take that TV cowboy ass-clown out with a smirk and a verbal stiff-arm without ever getting up off their bar stools. Tough is about being street-smart, and macho ain't gotta goddamn thing to do with it. Tough guys don't tell you how tough they are before they cave in your head.

Like my best friend, Jimmy, who was tougher than a truck-stop t-bone, but he never once put his badness out there unless you were dumb enough to test him.

Men like these are still around if ya know where to look. You order up some fancy-ass gin fizzy designer drink in this hell-hole, and when they're through laughing, odds are five-to-one or better you'll be clawing, begging, sassing and slugging your way back into the safety of the street.

Welcome to the Last Resort Inn, for my money the last stop on earth if ya still got a soft spot for tracking down the blood and guts of what little is left of America's soul.

A guy could get his ass killed in here, but at least you'd gasp your final heave-ho knowin' you got snuffed for all the right reasons. In here, ya get whatcha deserve. These cats can spot a phony at 50 paces, and even after throwin' down shots of rail in the double digits, they've still got instincts you can take to the fuckin' bank. There ain't no Jimmy Buffet on the jukebox at the Last Resort Inn, and you can take that to the bank, too.

I'm not one of 'em — not yet anyway — but lately, I've been getting the feeling that if this is rock bottom, maybe I wanna join the party after all. I've always been a big fan of rock bottom, but I never quite had the balls to give it the hairy eyeball and say, "FUCK IT. BRING IT ON!" I've dabbled in rock bottom, taunted it, teased it, caressed it, and even asked it to dance. But in the end, I was afraid. I still cared too much. I was holding out. But for what?

I always had to do something, be somewhere, chase a dream, chase a girl, chase my tail, prove myself — a pathetic overachiever. I was miserable, just another sucker in a world full of suction. I was a prisoner to my own warped agenda and the last to know — too busy chasing my life to live the fucker.

"You're only as rich as how ya spend your time, buddy boy," Jimmy had told me long ago. But I didn't get it then. I should've, though. Jimmy was lying on his deathbed at 33, an early victim of AIDS, and these were his final words to me before he checked in for good to the Other Side Hotel. Fuckin' Jimmy, man. Final words so golden they took a dozen years to sink in.

If ya wanna talk about your moment of clarity, buy me a shot of whiskey, and I'll tell ya all about it, brother. I've seen the light, and Jimmy was right on all along.

Rock bottom ain't no basement bargain after all. You learn your lessons wherever you can find 'em, but I'm starting to think that there's only so much wisdom to be found in a joint where whiskey makes the world go 'round.

In the end, it's not the booze that makes these geezers so dead on about shit. It's the lives they've led — dangerous and close to the bone. Hard drinkin' just makes it easier to tune out all the wicked scenes that wake you up in a cold sweat in the middle of the night. They drink so they don't give up. Okay, I can dig that. Bully for them if that's what works, cuz now I can finally see what Jimmy was trying to tell me all along.

You don't will yourself into the Last Resort Inn. You earn your goddamn pedigree the hard way when life has slapped the shit outta you so hard that you find yourself there whether you like it or not.

Still, I ain't that tough, so ya better keep that saloon door open, barkeep, just in case. I could be ready any old time ...

20

FAITH VS. THE PLANET EARTH

The man soared through the heavens, flying, really flying, at one with the sky, gliding effortlessly through the stratosphere like a god among gods, wrapped only in a cloak of delicate, wispy clouds.

The man smiled. He didn't need wings, no motorized magic; there was nothing but his faith to propel him. The sky creatures beheld him, curious, gathered around him, worshiping him and humming their sky creature sing song. Soon, he was the talk of the sky.

In measured earth time, the man had been soaring for three long months, although time was lost on the man. There was no thought, no sense of the miraculous and never even a hint of fear. There was only his flight, silent and timeless, like a child lost at play. The man was alone but never lonely, humble yet invincible. The man had the faith. Blind faith. Unshakeable faith. God-fearing faith.

Ironic isn't it that an unearthly thing like flying was the result of an earthly phenom that the ground creatures liked to call love?

It was over almost as suddenly as it had begun. The man spiraled downward in lazy, gentle arcs at first — picking up speed until he was plummeting towards earth at twice the speed of sound — a spent rocket on a crash course with ground zero. A million miles, 500,000, 200,000,100,000, 75,000. Downward. Faster and faster. Tumbling and twirling, vibrating in wild, out-of-control gyrations.

He still had the faith. Blind faith. Unshakable faith. God-fearing faith.

Down. Down. Down. Still no fear. He was free from harm.

At 50,000 feet, he reentered the earth's atmosphere. It hit him right between the eyes, like a jolt from a live wire. His earthly emotions returned to him in a frenzied flood, overloading his circuitry.

They were all there, familiar as a former friend. Jealousy. Paranoia. Guilt. Rage. Insecurity. Doubt. Suspicion. Panic. Loneliness. Isolation. Pride.

The impact was spectacular, gory as any plane crash, and a huge crowd of morbid fun-seekers gravitated to the scene to gawk at the victim's scattered remains. There were shattered limbs and deep pools of blood and shredded organs and shattered teeth and popped-out eyeballs. The man bled profusely through all eight orifices. He was dead before he hit the ground, smothered by his own humanity.

But isn't this funny? The one thing the man never allowed himself to feel was regret. The man had flown, he had really flown, and he rode that faith straight into the ground. Blind Faith. Unshakeable faith. God-fearing faith.

When I'm Depressed

in a world of suction i get sucked right in
it's so easy to blow it when you get sucked in
in a world of friction i get rubbed the wrong way
that's why i always blow up
when i don't get my way
columbus was wrong the world ain't round
it's just a world full of squares designed to bring me down
it's a cartoon world yeah my world's all my own
my teeth are the whitest so how come i'm alone?
everything fades to black
when i'm depressed
everything pisses me off
when i'm depressed
i get obsessed
when i'm depressed
i feel possessed
when i'm depressed
you ain't got a foggy notion why you're so depressed
you're the last one to know it when you're life is a mess
you been banished forever from the tinfoil people's club
black-balled from a world you want nuthin' from
i don't want nuthin' from it
put it right here
in a world divided it's always me against them
ya get the door open and it just gets slammed
you never get invited to where the shiny people go
ya feel so strip naked in your second hand clothes
everything fades to black
when i'm depressed
everything pisses me off
when i'm depressed
i get obsessed
when i'm depressed
i feel possessed
when i'm depressed
everything fades to black.

21

SORRY, THAT WASN'T ME
(CONFESSIONS OF A MANIC-DEPRESSIVE)

November 11, 2010

The mania raged non-stop for six straight months, a relentless euphoria. Decisions, if you could call them that, were made on a dime. Push the envelope and dodge the shrapnel. I was in-fucking-vincible. No kill switch and no sense of boundaries, blurting whatever raced through my ticker-tape brain. I was in orbit, spinning out of control and into the abyss, and everybody knew it.

Except for me of course.

When the mania kicks in, sorry bro, but you're just along for the ride, a mere passenger in your own spun-out life. I was in the moment, the toast of the town, on top of my game and nothing but nothing was beyond my grasp. Anything and everything was there for the taking. "Hey you, come here." I wanted it all, and I knew how to get it. I was the smartest, cockiest, wittiest, sexiest, most charming motherfucker in the room.

Any room.

Looking back on it now, I was a punchline.

More bourbon, more weed, more whatever ya got and "hey man, who's that little redhead over by the jukebox?" Two minutes later, I was on her like an assassin, overwhelming her with the world according to Robbie. She recoiled in horror, but I didn't notice. In my addled brain, she was already mine. My temper was hair-trigger, and if some loser got popped in the teeth in the process, so fuckin' be it, it was all in a night's work.

I was all about the action, and life was a bowl of goddamn cherries just begging to be devoured in one mighty gulp.

Seventeen thousand miles of chasing sprint car racing all over the country later, I'd blown 12 grand, lost the love of my life, been fired from my ten-year gig as a feature writer and columnist for an international racing magazine and gotten banned indefinitely from a racetrack that had been my second home since the year I graduated from high school. Hero to zero in one lost summer. In August, I wadded up my motorcycle when a wheelie went awry and severely burned my leg. Two days later, I blew up the motor.

The good times kept right on rolling. By summer's end, I'd been hit with two disorderly conducts, broken my hand in a fistfight in Alabama, acquired more than $600 in traffic tickets, been banned from attending any races from coast to coast by a governing sprint car entity called the World of Outlaws, banged a female cop in Georgia who agreed to leave her guns on, had my Jeep towed, gotten heave-hoed from countless bars, spent nearly four thousand on a record that may never be released, decked a club owner, gained 15 pounds and managed to lose both of my bands and most of my friends.

My life was in shambles, but I still couldn't see it.

My third manic episode in just seven years, and exactly like the experts tell you, bipolar disease only gets worse with age. I was already an anomaly in that I wasn't even diagnosed until I was 43, but as I look back on it now, your average 7-year-old boy doesn't get into fistfights twice a month or bang their friends into barbed wire fences while racing tricycles. I was mean and menacing. I still had a heart, but just barely.

The cycles come closer together and increase in severity. Despite the danger, the onset of mania is a welcome reprieve from the black hole of soul-crushing depression. You think you've got the world by the gonads, and you're sure that nothing can stop you.

Never mind that it's all a cruel illusion. The stats speak for themselves. If left untreated, 20% of manic-depressives off themselves, and thousands more end up in prison. Happy endings are as rare as sunshine in Hell.

Six months of hard living had taken its toll on my health. I'm much too old to withstand this kind of sustained physical abuse. Every day was another hangover. My stomach burned constantly, and I was eating Rolaids by the fistful. I developed a sinus infection and a death rattle cough that lasted well over a month. I was throwing up blood nearly every day, and I had to endure painful periodontal surgery that took six weeks to heal. I was a medical mess, and as if that wasn't enough, I was chronically smoking spice, synthetic weed, that only added to my emotional disorientation.

If you had the misfortune of crossing my path between April and September of 2010, I more than likely pissed you off, scared you, insulted you, alienated you, terrified you, offended you or repulsed you.

Sorry, man; that wasn't me.

At least you could avoid me, block me on Facebook, not take my frantic calls or throw me away altogether. I can't say I blame you. I was way beyond being reasoned with. The many people I'd wronged didn't care why. You don't get a pass just cuz you happen to be in the grips of an invisible illness that you have no control over. But I still was far from ready to admit that treatment was the only option that I had left.

Unless I wanted to die.

When the inevitable crash hits, and IS inevitable, somehow it always sneaks up on you. You know it's coming, but somehow you're never quite ready for it. The reversal is all but instantaneous — you simply shut down. Fun-time is over until all you see is the wreckage that you've left behind. The gray and the black envelops you, pressing in hard from all sides, a bolt from the blue free-fall into the darkest depths of hopelessness and despair.

It's over, and you're all but paralyzed.

The word "depression" doesn't even begin to do it justice. It's far, far worse than that. Life is stripped of all meaning, and simple daily tasks become insurmountable. There is no beauty, and there is no joy. Your dignity and grace are nowhere to be found.

You're all used up, eaten alive by guilt, fatigue and anxiety. Self-esteem, so disarmingly high a mere month ago, nosedives to new depths of self-loathing, and you disappear into a world of sleep, isolation and oldies television. You find yourself longing for childhood, warm mommy and hero daddy. I even stopped listening to or playing music. That's when I know I've hit the glass bottom, the end of the rope. When you take inventory and question whether or not life is worth living, you're pretty sure it isn't. Suddenly, I sucked at everything, and on the rare occasion when my phone rang, I couldn't even be bothered with answering it.

Nothing mattered anymore. Inside, I was already dead.

So now what?

In mid-March, I started seeing a psychiatrist and to no one's surprise, including my own, I was classified as bipolar one, a severe case. I quit drinking, stopped smoking dope and reluctantly put my fate into the hands of medical science. Nobody wants to be defined by their illness, but at least I'd finally accepted that the time had come to own up to it. Finding the proper combination of meds is an educated guess at best and a constantly moving target. It's a slow, painful process, and there are no miracle cures. No matter how strong your resolve, manic-depression cannot be willed away.

It's hell to admit it to you or anybody, but it's a fucking war I'll never, ever win. At 57, I'm starting over (again), completely from scratch. For the rest of my life, I'm stuck with taking ever-changing doses of antidepressants and mood stabilizers to save me from myself. And now, I'm just trying to find that elusive balance. At this point, I'll settle for just being gray.

Update

On Jan. 21, 2014, I came within a breath or two from becoming a bipolar statistic. I swallowed 50 or 60 Depakote and Seroquel and headed into the shower and tried to stab myself in the heart with a barber's scissors. When that proved futile, I slashed my left arm from my wrist to my elbow. I lost two pints of blood and left a gaping wound behind that took almost a year to heal, putting my life as a pro drummer in serious peril.

Through a series of phone calls from concerned friends, I was found comatose and borderline psychotic, and taken to the Milwaukee County Health Complex, where I remained for six weeks. On the way to the hospital with my dear friend, Jackie, I heard beautiful soul music that wasn't really there. Or was it?

Thanks to the love and attention I received from family and friends, I am here to tell my story and am pleased to report that I have not had a serious bout of mania or depression since. All I can do now is never let my guard down and keep the faith. The following is my suicide note, written to and for the lost love of my life.

Goodbye

death's a mere breath away
every breath i breathe is about you
every beat of my heart is without you
heaven's a shot away
every death i'll die is about you
heaven's one prayer away
everyday i'm living without you
(is about you)
heaven needs to make up her mind
every breath i take is without you
i know it doesn't matter to you
i'm one leap closer to death
one step closer to god
what the hell?
i've got no excuse
what the hell's the use?
i'm one step closer to you.
one step nearer to you.

Lyrics

I'm Empty Handed Again

i can't stop this high-speed, head-on crash
dreams get dashed when you're too slow to react
got my hands jammed deep down in my pockets
ain't got no dough to buy you chocolates

i'm empty handed again

i crack like glass, and you always get the best of me
i shine like ice in my sea of misery
got the will, but i ain't got the ticket
i should give you my life, but i only got a minute

i'm empty handed again

even the tin man's heart is beating
the whole world screams for the love we're seeking
the sounds of silence, can you feel your heart stop?
the weary world weeps for the love we've lost

i don't think i can lose my deceit
my head ya know, it's harder than old concrete
and baby i could write you a sexy love letter
i won't mean a word, but i'll feel better

got my hands jammed deep down in my pockets
ain't got no dough to buy you chocolates
i got the will but i ain't got the ticket
i should give you my life but i only got a minute

and honey that's me with a heart like a lion
when you're through with me, i still won't die

i'm empty handed again.

Daddy's Only Dreaming

mommy flashing red lights
daddy waving white flags
do ya smell trouble?
no i only smell a rat
pink tights hot flesh
burning from the wicked stench
mommy flashing red lights
daddy burning white flags

so ya got a private audience
she already in the past tense
she so catholic
she so tense
you ain't hard and she ain't wet
a stand-in dummy gonna take your place
another song and dance to face
do i sound bitter?
do i sound harsh?
another stuffed shirt with too much starch

another lousy bleeding heart
get out quick if you're so smart
i see you shudder
did i touch a nerve?
i'm straight up, i just missed a curve
do i sound bitter?
do i sound bold?
i'm bruised and battered and beaten and old
do i seem shattered?
do i seem cold?
i'm a brand new scene from the same old show

a beach bum basking in the snow
pay the piper with playtime dough
melt her down until she froze
i'll pay my money and not pass go
mommy running red lights
daddy burning bridges

daddy only dreaming
he only wants to melt you down
don't kick that sleeping dog
he only wants to burn you down
daddy only dreaming.

I'm the Eraser

you're the paper
and i'm the eraser
here comes that white girl
and i can't face her

an iron in the fire
one horse in the race
here comes that white girl
she has no face

a ring on her finger
chains on her feet
she's out of my life
without missing a beat

baby sure cured me
sure cured me of that
i know you can sink
even lower than that

you're the paper and i'm the eraser
here comes that white girl
i still can't face her

i'm gonna rub you out
i'm gonna rub you out
i'm gonna rub you out
you're just blank paper
and i'm the eraser

About the Author

I was born and bred in Mt. Pleasant, Iowa (pop. 7,513), the live-wire son of an ultra-driven but hard-drinking savings and loan executive and a hyperactive perfectionist with a cleaning fetish who had once been voted "America's Most Beautiful Teenager." Believe me when I tell ya my mother, Alice, was a real show-stopper in the looks department — china doll skin, long, shapely legs, willow wasp waist and all.

We had a lousy county fair, a state institution for the mentally deranged — (my mother told me they had people in there who ate their own poop) — a highly regarded high school football program, and our tallest building was three stories high. We even had a Dairy Queen. There were eleven bars. Drunken lushes everywhere I looked.

For the first 14 years of my life, we were a racing town, which suited me just fine. But Mt. Pleasant, then as now, can't do anything right. With the stroke of a city planner's pen, racing was abolished without fanfare in 1968. This was the first of many grudges that I still hold against my hometown. One day, I swear I will burn the president of the fair board's house to the fucking ground (not really) to get even with him for this unspeakable crime against humanity. The once mighty half-mile Iowa top-soil oval has now been reduced to hosting tractor pulls and demolition derbies once a year during our pathetic county fair. Dirty bastards.

For a kid like me, who craved non-stop action and cheap thrills, the small town pace felt like slow death. Me and my best friend, Joe Rommel, great-nephew of the Desert Fox, Erwin Rommel, engaged in constant rounds of malicious vandalism and grand larceny capers. Brushes with the cops became commonplace.

Mt. Pervert, as my friends and I liked to call it, used to be known as a nice, squeaky clean place to raise a family — a regular Norman Rockwell painting sprung to life.

But not anymore.

In the span of just 12 years, there were 15 homicides, most of them unsolved, easily the most notorious of which was the point-blank assassination of our mayor at a city council meeting in 1985. I'd known Edd King all my life, and he was a prince of a man if ever there was one. Whacked-out World War II vet Ralph Oren Davis (how come assassins always have three names?) was unhappy that his sewer was backing up, and when the meeting was called to order, Davis approached the dais and started blasting. Put a woman in my mom's bridge club in a wheelchair for life. Davis, I hope, is still rotting in prison in nearby Fort Madison.

Suddenly, meth labs were as plentiful as pig shit, and these tweaked-out thugs would shoot you in the face over a rack of 8-ball. I just had to get the fuck outta there and fast.

After a four-and-a-half-year stint at a cow college in Missouri armed me with a bachelor's degree, I began my first real stab at becoming a responsible citizen in Champaign, Illinois. This proved to be a complete debacle.

Convinced that certain pop stardom was my destiny, me and my beloved '59 Ludwigs migrated to Milwaukee's burgeoning punk scene, where my services were enlisted as drummer and singer for such notable acts as RPMs, Red Ball Jets, Plasticland, Liquid Pink, Dog-Style Dandies, The Carolinas, White-Hot Tizzies, Love Bully, Rob McCuen and the Ruins, and countless other bad-ass, fly-by-night combos.

At last count, I have plied my trade in 29 states and 14 countries on rock and roll's dime, and have appeared either as singer or drummer on 23 records.

My life's work now lives in bargain bins all over the world.

All the while, my musical "career" has been repeatedly interrupted by the annoying reality of earning a living, an endeavor in which I continue to fail miserably. In the 31 jobs I have been force-fed throughout my slapstick life, there is but one common denominator: They all sucked.

Rob McCuen

www.ingramcontent.com/pod-product-compliance
Lightning Source LLC
Chambersburg PA
CBHW020921140626
46545CB00015B/1107